Haiden C. Trigg

The American Fox-Hound

Embracing a History of the celebrated Trigg, Birdsong and Maupin Strains

Haiden C. Trigg

The American Fox-Hound
Embracing a History of the celebrated Trigg, Birdsong and Maupin Strains

ISBN/EAN: 9783337180300

Printed in Europe, USA, Canada, Australia, Japan

Cover: Foto ©ninafisch / pixelio.de

More available books at **www.hansebooks.com**

———THE ———

AMERICAN FOX-HOUND

BY

HAIDEN C. TRIGG.

(FULL CRY)

Embracing a History of the Celebrated Trigg, Birdsong and Maupin Strains.

PRICE $1.25.

HAIDEN C. TRIGG, GLASGOW, KY.
Originator of the Trigg Red Fox Dog.

PREFACE.

I have received of late years so many letters from parties who have come into possession of what has become known as the Trigg Dog, and from others desiring to secure them, that I have at last decided to write this book, intended as a brief history of my dogs and those of Messrs. Birdsong and Maupin from which the Trigg Dog originated. I shall be brief, confining myself to facts gathered from my personal acquaintance with both Mr. Birdsong and Mr. Maupin and their dogs, and from my numerous correspondence with these and other famous lovers of the chase, extending over thirty-five years. Some of the letters I have submitted herewith, believing they would be interesting and instructive to the new generation of sportsmen.

I have the greatest confidence in the strains mentioned herein, but the different modes of hunting the fox in various sections require certain qualities to predominate; then, there are "as many men of many minds" as there are dogs of "high and low degree."

I believe, after twenty-five years acquaintance with them, during which time I have tested their speed, nose, hunting qualities, etc., with representative dogs from nearly every famous pack of the country, and from the evidence of their worth as testified to by many letters from those who have run them after various game in other States, that I have a strain of dogs at least as good as those of their famous ancestors or any of to-day. I know from almost daily experience that I can run to earth or catch the red fox.

To those of you who have my dogs, and to you who have other strains, we invite correspondence. I will be glad to exchange information, experiences, etc.

Jan. 1, 1890. HAIDEN C. TRIGG.

CONTENTS.

The Author (Illustration)	3
Preface	5
Red Fox Horn (Illustration)	9
The Chase	11
Business (Illustration)	17
Old and Modern Hounds	19
Gray Fox Horn (Illustration)	21
George L. F. Birdsong (Illustration)	25
"Uncle Wash" Maupin (Illustration)	29
Birdsong and Maupin Dogs	34
Letters from Famous Hunters	36
"Dick's Dog" (Illustration)	37
Jake (Illustration)	51
Annie (Illustration)	65
H. C. Trigg's Residence (Illustration)	69
National Meet (Illustration)	73
Buying and Selling	79
Death of Hornet	77
Description of Dogs	81
Ned (Illustration)	85
The Full Cry Pack	87
Twenty-four Years Ago	94
Full Cry Hounds (Illustration)	95

RED FOX HORN.

W. J. Morton, Weatherford, Tex., to H. C. Trigg, Glasgow, Ky.

THE CHASE.

"Independent of the pleasure arising from the chase I have always considered a covert side, with hounds that are well attended, to be one of the most lively scenes in nature. The pride of the morning, the meeting of friends, and the anticipation of diversion, contributes to raise the spirits and expand the soul."

The English people, for centuries, have indulged in the fox chase and have spent thousands of pounds for the improvement of the hound.

Our ancestors who settled in Virginia and Maryland brought over with them the love of the chase which, at an early day, permeated the States of Georgia, the Carolinas, Kentucky and Tennessee. The sportsmen of these States, in ante-bellum days, were lavish in their expenditures on the improvement of the fox-hound. I think our best strains of dogs to-day are equal, if not superior, to the English, for this country. This, I know, is a bold assertion, and may be challenged, but 'tis said that experience is the best of teachers.

I have owned and seen many imported dogs, but have yet to see one the superior or equal of our best American animals. This country requires a different dog from England. There, the land is nearly all in a high state of cultivation; the coverts are small and the atmospheric conditions more favorable for holding the scent. The hunters ride to these small covert sides where the fox is known to be located and find him. With us we must have dogs of superior nose and better ranging qualities, that will go a great distance in our immense woodlands in quest of the game. The large English hound of the same speed in the open would be outfooted by our smaller American dog in the brier-fields and heavy undergrowth of our forests.

The late turfman, Mr. Harper, was once asked the first requisite of a race horse. "Speed," he answered. "What next?" "More speed," he replied. Not so with the fox-hound; he must possess other qualities—ranging, good nose, with judgment, a good tongue, true to the line and *dead game*. The National Fox Hunters' Association has recently adopted a standard for the American fox-hound. It is certainly pleasing to the eye and desirable to see a pack uniform in size and color, but as nearly all the best packs in this country are owned and maintained by individuals, it will be some years before we can hope to breed with any certainty of getting this standard. Few beginners realize the time, trouble and expense it requires to breed, rear or get together a pack of well broke hounds, that can and will kill or drive to earth the red fox in from one to three hours. To begin with, the greatest care and good judgment should be exercised in selecting breeders. None but dogs of known ancestry, whose gameness and speed have been tried and tested with others of reputation, should be bred. We put gameness and speed first, but there are other qualities almost as important. The breeders should be sound in limb, perfectly healthy, and free of blemishes, with ranging qualities, a good nose and true to the line. It is not always possible to find these requisites combined, as they should be, in one dog, but breed so as to get these as near as possible, and at the same time try to eliminate the objectionable traits. If you have a bitch that is deficient in any one of these qualities you should select for your stud dog one that surpasses in this respect. Thus, by paying close attention to these selections one can, in time, produce with almost a certainty the standard, or his ideal dog.

I do not advocate too close in-breeding, though I have known instances of very satisfactory results from such. My Georgia friends, during the sixties, thought so much of the dog "July" that they in-bred him extensively. The result has been the perpetuation of his good points to an amazing extent, and produced a type differing from the dogs of the same parent strain.

I have tried the same experiment in breeding "Forest" to one of his get, and although I have raised five of the puppies the result was not satisfactory, none proving equal to either sire or dam. The second or third generations were more satisfactory.

If possible, the young dog should be reared under your own supervision. For ten years I have made it a rule to always be present when the dogs were fed, or rather to feed them myself, and by so doing I gained the affections of my pack, and saw that the more timid ones got their share of the rations. If you wish your kennel well attended, do it yourself; if half-done, get a good man to do it for you.

Feed regularly on wholesome food. The youngster can be injured as much by overfeeding with strong rations as by not being fed enough. A puppy fed entirely on meat, or the refuse of a slaughter pen, will develop an abnormal neck and head, and become awkward in his actions. After they become old enough to roam, they should be unrestrained. The hound requires more exercise to keep him in condition than any other species of the dog family. The puppy should be encouraged to chase rabbits as soon as they will give tongue on the trail, and later should be hunted for the gray fox before trying him on a red. This exercise is necessary for the proper development of the body and the education of the young dog.

Never raise a puppy by himself. I have frequently taken such in my kennels when fifteen or eighteen months old, and it took time and trouble to get them to bark to the pack. If in the country on a farm with hay ricks, straw stacks, shuck pens, out houses, etc., the dog should be allowed to select his own sleeping-place, which he will change often—as sleeping in the same place for a long time without change of bedding will develop disease and vermin. If confined, their beds can not be changed too often.

You must exercise great discretion in training young dogs. The experienced sportsman will detect any peculiar traits when first taken to the field. After a few chases, some youngsters will at once abandon rabbits and other game and give tongue only on the fox's trail, while others will persist in hunting and giving mouth to all kind of game. Patience must be exercised with this latter class. Some will require severe punishment, while others can be taught best by persuasion. It is a sure sign of a good dog for the puppy to begin hunting early and keep it up persistently.

In taking the young dog after his first red fox, it is important that you have well-trained dogs in your pack, that will cry nothing but the game desired. The puppy will soon learn their tongues, and, relying on them, will abandon his rabbit and hearken to the first challenge.

Silence and patience are the two essential qualifications of the sportsman. Above all things, learn to govern yourself. Hallooing and sounding the horn is indulged in too much by many of the sportsmen. Often have I known men who owned quite handsome packs start out in the morning by blowing their horns and constantly hallooing and keeping up the noise during the entire day. The result is the fox is off before the dogs get up to him, and such packs are noisy and riotous in imitation of their masters. Learn to keep your mouth shut, and only give vent to your feelings when spontaneous and you can not keep it.

Much injustice is done dogs by hunting them and expecting a run on cold, wintry days, often when the ground is frozen and the conditions altogether unfavorable. There being no scent, the dogs can not possibly carry the trail. They are then criticised, when really the hunters or master is at fault. Our Kentucky climate is not very favorable for hunting. I average not more than one good day in seven during the hunting season. The best time for the hunt is early in the morning, when the ground is damp and the temperature not below freezing. The atmosphere should be heavy, with a light southern breeze and a cloudy sky. On such a morning, the pack will run with heads up and sterns down, and will not have to straddle the trail. Get to the covert by daylight, or as soon thereafter as possible; keep quiet until the game is up and running; then, if practicable, ride with your dogs, not getting close enough to interfere with the scent. If the country is such that you are unable to follow, ride to the known crossing.

Some prefer night hunting, but to me the sight of the fox, followed by a pack of fleet hounds in full cry, is the most exciting scene imaginable. But if you can not spare the time to hunt during the day, night hunting has some decided advantages. In the country I have no diversions, such as theaters, lectures and other entertainments, enjoyed by city folks, so I can spend the long winter evenings in the enjoyment of the chase. The cry made by hounds at night sounds much more musical than by day; the fox stands up longer; the atmospheric conditions are better; the dogs make fewer faults; stock is at rest, and the game is not so wild and more readily found. The fox or dogs are not often seen, but the trained ear of the experienced sportsman knows the tongue of every dog in his pack, and by the way it is given can almost to a certainty place their positions in a race on the darkest night.

In this State I have one trouble in killing the fox which is experienced in no other State, to the same extent. A red fox is familiar with every burrow in his territory, which is usually from five to ten miles in extent. Kentucky is so honeycombed with these safe retreats that the fox is at all times in easy reach of some one of them. Frequently, when fairly beaten, he saves his life by taking refuge in one of these numerous holes or caverns, yet I often kill in the open.

I am sometimes amused at our Northern friends thinking that we could neither kill or drive to earth the red fox. Some months ago I received a letter from a member of the Chicopee Fox Club, of Chicopee, Massachusetts, saying: "I have never yet seen a Southern fox-hound worth the powder to blow his brains out." This gentleman and his club have certainly been imposed upon by some of the unreliable dog dealers to be found all over the country. Never get a dog **from a man unless he be a practical and reliable sportsman.**

We would say to our Massachusetts friend in particular, and our Northern friends in general, get on a train and come South, and see for yourselves. You will find the latchstring hanging on the outer wall of every fox hunter in Kentucky, whether he lives in a log cabin or a brick or a stone mansion.

The mode and object of hunting the fox in the South differs materially from that of the North. Our style partakes more of the English; we use horses that will and do take fences and stone walls. They are bred to stand our hard, cross-country riding. I delight in the chase itself, and take every means possible to protect the game, never killing unless fairly caught in the open by the dogs. In the North, where the red fox is more plentiful, the greater pleasure of the chase seems to be in shooting the game. This mode of killing sounds strange to the ears of the Southern sportsman. It is claimed that foxes are so plentiful there and change so often on the dogs that it is difficult to kill or drive them to earth with their dogs. A few years ago, I received a letter from a gentleman north of the Ohio, who claims to be a great lover of the chase and advertises his strain of dogs extensively. In replying to him, I made inquiry as to his mode of hunting, whether his country was a good one to ride over, and did he have horses that were trained to take fences. Replying to my inquiry he said that he "*usually hunted in a buggy.*" I dropped his letter in the waste-basket and never replied. Only an octogenarian could be excused for such a turnout.

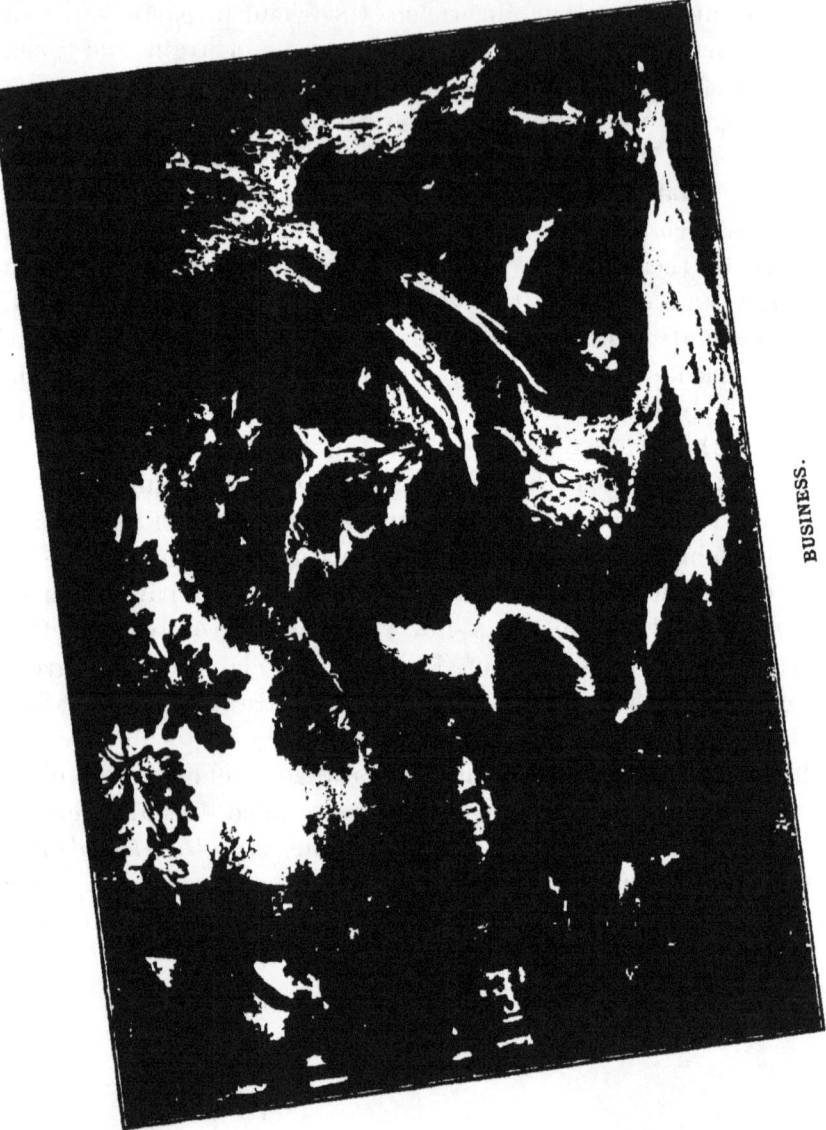

BUSINESS.

OLD AND MODERN HOUNDS.

From 1845 to 1860 I owned a pack of those grand old long-eared, rat-tail, deep-toned, black-and-tan Virginia fox hounds. In those happy, bygone days I could on a moonlight night ride to the covert side, throw my leg over the pommel of my saddle and listen for hours to the most magnificent music made by the ever-to-be-remembered dogs.

But, alas, everything must have an end. In 1860 the red fox first made his advent into my section and the days of these dogs were ended. The coming of the red fox made a great change in the chase. The most important thing was to get a dog that could successfully walk with him. With me it required years of work, patience, considerable expense, and a world of trouble to gather the desired pack. I am now on the shady side of life and will soon have to bow to the inevitable. That my strain of dogs, of which I feel a right to be proud, may be preserved, I have consented to give a brief history of them to the sportsmen of America, believing that by great care in selecting, judicious breeding, and constant hunting for the past thirty-five years, I have produced a dog that can successfully compete with the red fox.

In 1866, I opened correspondence with George L. F. Birdsong, of Thomaston, Georgia, and purchased of him that year and in 1867 the following dogs, paying these prices:

```
CHASE AND BEE (by Longstreet) ............$100.00
GEORGE ................................. 100.00
RIP .................................... 100.00
FANNIE ................................. 100.00
```

Lee was presented to me.

In 1868, I visited Mr. Birdsong and spent a week with him. He was then in feeble health, in fact threatened with that terrible disease, consumption, from which he died the 18th of August the following year.

He was able to take me on but one hunt, when we caught a red fox in forty-five minutes. I suspected the fox was not in condition to run, and held a *post mortem*, but found nothing wrong with him.

Mr. Birdsong then had in his kennel—we had him in the hunt—a dog that has been talked about a great deal in late years, "July." We also had in the pack three of his get, I think then about three years old, *i. e.*: "Madcap," "Lightfoot" and "Echo." He also had three yearlings out of "Echo" by his celebrated dog, "Longstreet," *i. e.*: "Delta," "Dumas," and "David." By begging two days and paying five hundred dollars ($500) he let me have "Lightfoot" and "Delta." In addition to these I purchased of Colonel R. H. Ward, of Green county, Georgia, "Forest," by "Boston," paying one hundred dollars, and "Emma" at the same figures. "Rose," a full sister to Echo, by July, and "Hampton," were loaned me. Rose, I returned after she whelped, but Hampton died in my kennel a few months after I received him.

In 1867 I visited General G. W. Maupin, of Madison county, Kentucky, and was present at the great match race between Ben Robinson, of Montgomery county and General Maupin. This meet took place at the Oil Spring, in Clark county, and was much talked about by the hunters everywhere at that time.

After the race I accompanied General Maupin home, spending several days hunting with him. On my departure I purchased of him a young bitch called "Minnie," that was one or two crosses from his celebrated dog, "Tennessee Lead," on one side and the imported English dogs on the other. Colonel C. J. Walker at the same time gave me a young bitch called "Mattie," the pedigree of which is the same as that seen in Colonel Walker's letter herein. Both of these were proud, magnificent fox-hounds.

In 1869, I visited W. L. Waddy and Thomas Ford of Shelby county, who had a splendid pack of the Maupin strain of dogs.

I hunted some days with these gentlemen. Mr. Waddy was so well pleased with my dogs that he requested me on my departure to take some of his best dogs with me and test their qualities. I selected three, i. e., "Tip," "Waxy," and his celebrated dog, "One Eyed King." This last dog was closely related to Mr. Maupin's "Lead" and the English importation of 1857. I hunted these dogs about six months. The dog "King" was a wonderful animal for speed, and dead game, though deficient in nose. I crossed him on Delta (by Longstreet out of Echo by July) and succeeded in raising two puppies, a dog and a bitch. The dog I kept and called "Money." He was the fastest dog I ever owned, but not so game as others of my pack. The bitch puppy I sent to Mr. Waddy and he called her "Echo." She proved to be superior to anything in Mr. Waddy's pack. The following year Mr. Waddy and Thomas Ford paid me a visit. On their return I let them take my celebrated dog "Forest." They had some bitches served by him, the produce being, like that of King and Delta, superior to any dogs they had previously owned. I submit letters herewith bearing me out in these statements.

About four years ago I got of Mr. E. T. Halsey, of Louisville, an imported dog, "Portland," from the "Quorn Kennels," England. This dog, like all imported dogs that I have ever seen, was too large for our country. He was deficient in nose, speed and ranging qualities—in fact a failure. I bred him to a few of my bitches and the produce proved fairly good. I think by three or four crosses they will make fine animals. About the same time W. S. Walker, of Garrard County, Kentucky, was kind enough to send me one of his stud dogs, which I crossed on some of our best bitches, the produce proving very satisfactory. Mr. Walker is an experienced, practical sportsman, has a fine pack of dogs and is doing a great deal toward improving the fox-hound in Kentucky.

From 1867 to 1890 I have had in my kennel the following dogs, of the pure Birdsong, Maupin and Walker strains, which

I begged, borrowed and bought for the purpose of improving my pack;

MAUPIN'S	BIRDSONG'S	WALKER'S
MINNIE	CHASE	BUCKNER
MATTIE	BEE	SCOTT
LEAD	GEORGE	TROOPER
COUCHMAN	LIGHTFOOT	
BOB	DELTA	
DICK	RIP	
MILTON	FANNIE	
BLUCHER	LEE	
MAC	FOREST	
RAIBY (Called Redhead)	EMMA	
TIP	HAMPTON	
WAXEY	WARD	
ONE EYED KING	ROSE	
HAEFER'S DICK	EMMA SAMPSON	
ROCK		
VENUS		
MERCY		
LEE		
BRENDA		

General Maupin, the Walkers, Sam Martin, Gentrys, Whites and others of that section were honest in their belief that Fox, Rifler, Martin, Queen, Tennessee Lead, Tickler, Doc, Kate, Top, Towstring, Minnie and other famous dogs of their packs were superior to any dogs of their day.

Mr. Birdsong, the Wards, Robinsons, Ridgleys, Jacksons, and others of Georgia were equally as confident that Hodo, July, Longstreet, Flora, Forest, Echo, Hampton, Madcap, Lightfoot, Fannie, and others of their packs were the peers of any living dogs.

Mr. Waddy and Tom Ford of Shelby county, Kentucky, thought as well of their One Eyed King, Tip, Josephine,

GEO. L. F. BIRDSONG.

Venus, and others. W. S. Walker, whose letter is given, states his opinion as to the merits of Trooper.

I differ from some men who make the bold assertion that they have the best dogs on earth. Because a favorite dog runs in the lead of a certain pack does not warrant his admirers in stating he can beat all alike. Dogs are like race horses; they are the best until they meet their superiors. The true sportsman is never so prejudiced as not to admit that there may be other dogs equal to his own, and that by crossing on such dogs his strain would be improved.

GEORGE L. F. BIRDSONG.

Previous to our Civil War, no class of people were so fortunately situated as to indulge their taste and follow their inclinations as the Southern planter. The occupation of the planter was considered as honorable as any in the South. Professional men and statesmen had their plantations, embracing thousands of acres, and hundreds of slaves. They had certain incomes, lived up to them, indulging their tastes as fancy or inclination desired. They spent part of their winters in New Orleans or Cuba and their summers in the North. Many of them were educated at the best colleges of the country, were fine scholars and entertaining writers. They were not fond of manual labor, as there was never any necessity for it. They possessed certain traits that were never excelled by any people of ancient or modern times. Chesterfieldian in manners, they prized their word and honor above lucre or life. Their love and devotion to woman bordered on worship. George L. F. Birdsong was one of this class. His time, fortune and life were spent with books and field sports, until the beginning of the war, when his fortune was given to his country. He was a connoisseur on fox-hounds, bird dogs and fire-arms. He imported the first pair of red foxes from New York to this section of Georgia. He imported hounds from Maryland, Virginia and other States, when he would have to send wagons hundreds of miles for them, there being no railroads or express companies. If he lived to-day he would likely be called a crank. He would have his gun weigh seven pounds ten ounces—no more, no less. His fox horn was made of the tusk of an elephant and cost him $50.00. His hounds were of a certain carriage, peculiar marks, pedigreed and bred like the turfman does his horse. One of the characteristic marks of the Birdsong dog is a certain curl of the hair on the shoulder.

Around Thomaston, Georgia, Mr. Birdsong's home, the country was peculiarly adapted for the chase. Cleared fields embracing thousands of acres, no burrows or caves for the fox to take refuge in when hard pressed but which he could be dug out of in a short time. Dogs of no greater speed would kill a dozen foxes in such a country to one in Kentucky.

All of Birdsong's hunting was done in the daytime.

Soon after the Henry dogs were imported by him and he had demonstrated that they could kill the red fox, Mr. Birdsong was challenged by parties in a distant county that had a red fox which they said his dogs could not kill or drive to earth. He accepted the invitation and put his dogs in a wagon. Arriving at the place he found a great number of hunters and dogs galore. In the first day's hunt when the fox was being closely pressed some of the native hunters rocked Birdsong's dogs and the fox escaped. Mr. Birdsong was informed of this outrage. At the meet the next day he made the proposition that he would run his dogs only, and if he did not catch the fox he would acknowledge defeat. After a long discussion this was finally agreed to by the other hunters. The fox was easily found and after standing up a couple of hours was dead beat and took refuge in a sand bank. The hunters soon gathered, and Birdsong ordered his negro men

"UNCLE WASH" MAUPIN.

to go for a hoe and spade. Some of the native hunters declared he should not dig the fox out. Colonel R. H. Ward, of the county, was of the party, and seeing the great injustice being done Mr. Birdsong, he threateningly declared that the first man that interfered with the men digging, he would kill on the spot. In a short time Birdsong had the fox out, cut off his brush and handed him over to the hunters.

In consideration of this fair treatment by Colonel Ward, Mr. Birdsong, on his return home, sent him one of his best bitches, "Reel," or "Flora," from which Colonel Ward raised his best dogs. Mr. Birdsong was highly educated and a beautiful writer. His contributions to the *Countryman* were always interesting. His description of a fox chase was finer than any I ever read.

GEN. G. W. MAUPIN.

It was fortunate that "Uncle Wash" Maupin lived under the "old regime" in the long time ago 'befoh de wah."

His surroundings, the country and people, were congenial to one of his nature. The early settlers of Madison county were a noble class of men; their word was their bond. Such unselfish hospitality as existed in those happy, by-gone days, not only in Madison county but throughout Kentucky, will probably never be known again. Every neighborhood shared and shared alike when a beef or mutton was killed. No man thought of charging his neighbor for seed corn, potatoes, or garden seed. Many of those grand old men would have considered it an insult for a stranger to offer to pay for a night's lodging. The question is often discussed, "Do college bred men succeed best in life?" "Uncle Wash" not only never was in college, but never had the advantages of a log school house.

Notwithstanding this great disadvantage he fought the "battle of life" and won. He possessed very remarkable conversational powers and was always the central figure at the country gatherings. His home, comprising a thousand acres of Bluegrass land, was very appropriately called "The Hunter's Rest." The latchstring didn't hang on the outer wall like most of Kentucky homes for the reason that the doors always stood wide open to his numerous friends.

Physically, he was a magnificent specimen of manhood. When on the shady side of life he was yet as active as an athlete. Well do I remember the first hunt with him. We had started our fox and the dogs were out of hearing. Most of the party had followed the pack, but I remained with "Uncle Wash." We were riding as fast as our horses could carry us in order to intercept the dogs at a certain crossing. Suddenly "Uncle Wash" was off his horse, threw himse'f flat on the ground, with one side of his head pressed close to the earth and almost instantly he remounted and was off. No circus rider could have performed this feat more gracefully and in less time. After a ride of twenty minutes, under whip and spur, we were rewarded by the music of the pack coming over the mountains straight to us, when we witnessed the unusual sight of seeing fox and dogs at the same time, which called forth the view-halloo from both us. He was at home when mounted on a favorite horse, in the open field, ascending the mountain side, charging a snake fence or leaping dangerous ditches. He never knew fear or thought of danger. The expert English rider, mounted on his best hunter, the Arab of the far East, our own cowboy of the Western plains could not have followed Uncle Wash, Sam Martin and others of that clan, with a strong fox in front of such dogs at Tennessee Lead, Top, Tickler and others.

I shall never forget a sight witnessed when with Uncle Wash and a party of his friends on a hunt. We were passing through a large plantation. The question of horses and riders were being discussed, when George Maupin, a son of General

Maupin, challenged his cousin Seth Maupin, by making the remark, "You can not follow me."

"Give me your hand," said Seth. Instantly George threw out his left hand and Seth seizing it with his right, they drove spurs into their horses and made for a ten-rail stake and ridered fence, distant about three hundred yards. I shuddered when I saw them approaching the fence at such a speed. The collision could have been heard for a mile; riders and horses went over; rails flew in every direction. Seth Maupin was unhorsed but George kept his seat, and riding some hundred yards called back, "Can you follow me?" In the meantime, we had come up. While Seth was unhorsed, he escaped a scratch. George, although retaining his seat, received a severe cut across the forehead and was bleeding profusely. I said to his father, "Had George better not go home and see a physician?"

"No, son, that scratch is nothing; it will soon heal up, but there, he has broken one of Turner's rails that will never grow together."

Just then Tickler gave tongue about half a mile distant. Uncle Wash was off in an instant calling out, "Boys, put up that fence before you leave there." In half an hour the boys came up. George received no sympathy from any of the party on account of his hurt. It was looked upon as an ordinary occurrence.

It was never too cold or hot for "Uncle Wash" to ride twenty or thirty miles. When the ground was frozen, covered with snow and ice, the temperature to zero, he would build his fire on the side of a mountain and turn his dogs loose of a cloudy night and listen to them for hours. He required his dogs to follow the fox as long as he remained on top of ground. The tendons of such dogs were of iron and their nerves of steel.

BIRDSONG AND MAUPIN DOGS.

Of the men who have passed from the stage of life, none deserve the gratitude of the lovers of the chase more than George L. F. Birdsong of Georgia, and General Maupin, of Madison county, Kentucky.
In the early forties Dr. T. Y. Henry (grandson of Patrick Henry), of Virginia, presented George L. F. Birdsong, of Thomaston, Georgia, with a pair of puppies from his pack of hounds, which at that time had made an enviable reputation in Virginia. Mr. Birdsong sent a wagon overland (there being no railroad at that time) for the dogs. They proved to be superior to any dogs he had owned up to that time. In 1844 or 1845 Dr. Henry, being threatened with that dreaded disease, consumption, was ordered South by his physician. He started, traveling leisurely by wagon, accompanied by a party of friends, carrying his fine kennel of hounds with him, stopping at different points, putting in the time hunting and fishing as it suited their fancy. Mr. Birdsong, being informed of his movements, intercepted Dr. Henry en route, spending some days with him.
On reaching Florida, the deer being plentiful, Dr. Henry's dogs frequently ran them, when they would always take to the bayous and lagoons. When swimming after the game the dogs would be killed by alligators that infested these waters. Dr. Henry soon realized that his much-prized pack would be exterminated if something was not done. He wrote the facts to his friend, Mr. Birdsong, telling him that he might have the remnant of his famous pack if he would come after them. Mr. Birdsong, while sympathizing with his friend in his misfortune, was glad of an opportunity to secure these much-coveted dogs, and at once started for them.
Dr. Henry called them Irish hounds, they being descendants of "Mountain" and "Muse," imported from Ireland by

Bolton Jackson, of Maryland, and presented by him to Captain Sterret Ridgley. He gave them to Governor Ogle, of Maryland. He gave Mountain to Captain Charles Carroll, of Carrollton. He gave him to Dr. Buchannan, and he gave Captain (a direct descendant of Mountain and Muse) to Dr. Henry. See Turf Register Col. 3, pp. 287, 350 and 403 Vol. 4, pp. 234 and 397. This was the foundation of the celebrated Birdsong dogs. In 1861 the famous dog, "July," imported into Georgia by Miles G. Harris, who purchased him of Gosnell, of Maryland, was crossed on the Birdsong dogs. From letters in my possession and private conversation with Mr. Birdsong, I am satisfied that this dog "July" was of the same strain of old "Captain" and the original Henry dogs.

These dogs were called "Irish hounds" by Dr. Henry. Mr. Birdsong insisted they be known as the "Henry hounds," but they became famous as the Birdsong strain. Since the importation of the dog "July" and the death of Mr. Birdsong they have been called indiscriminately the "July hound."

The sportsmen of Georgia will pardon me for expressing the opinion that the name "July" should never have been substituted for "Birdsong." I am aware of the fact that a great difference of opinion existed among the sportsmen of Georgia as to the relative merits of the dogs after the crossing of them on July. "Longstreet" and "Hodo" were strictly Birdsong dogs, having no cross of July in them unless through the original importation of the dogs Mountain and Muse.

I owned and hunted the get of both Longstreet and July and have my opinion of the relative merits of their produce.

In the early fifties General Maupin and his friends imported many dogs from South Carolina, Virginia and Maryland, sparing no expense to improve their stock. In 1857 they imported from England, I think, three dogs, "Fox," "Rifler" and "Marth." About this time General Maupin got from East Tennessee the dog "Tennessee Lead," which he, Maupin, thought the best dog he ever owned. The cross of the English dogs, and especially the "Lead" cross on their previous importations produced a dog which has justly become famous, and was known as the "Maupin dog." This strain has been preserved and bred with great care by W. S. Walker & Bros., of Garrard county, Kentucky, and are known today as the Walker dogs.

LETTERS OF FAMOUS HUNTERS.

I publish a few of the very many letters I have on file. Some of them are from friends long since passed from us, but whose names were well known to every lover of the chase throughout the South in "the days before the war." Their reputations live after them and are honored by many of to-day. I would be glad to furnish more of these letters from such famous hunters, especially those of Mr. Birdsong, Dr. Henry and Colonel Ward, but my space will not admit. Some of these letters will prove interesting reading. They are instructive and full of history and especially so to the younger sportsmen, who are interested in the red fox and the red-fox hound:

DRYFORK, KY., August 1, 1895.

H. C. Trigg.

Yours of the 28th ult. received with check for fifty dollars in full payment of the hound "Rattler," better known as "Dick's Dog." I would not have parted with this dog had I not been worried so much by parties sending bitches to be bred to him. I consider him to be the best fox-hound I ever owned, and he is so considered by every fox hunter that has seen him in the field. He is a better ranger, trailer, and possesses greater speed than his sire, Jim Sibbins, that you sent to Texas. All of his puppies have proved to be fine dogs. He is now about eight years old. 'Tis needless for me to say

"DICK'S DOG." JIM SIBBINS—NORA.

anything about his breeding; you know his pedigree better than I do.
                              Yours truly,
                                   DICK SMITH.

————

                         QUINCY, FLA., ——— 15, 1867.
H. C. Trigg, Glasgow, Ky.,

DEAR SIR: Yours of the 9th inst. to hand, and I reply at once. I have had a stroke of paralysis which incapacitates me for writing, being compelled to use my left hand. I consider my dogs without a peer. They have been bred with as much scrupulousness and exactness as the race horse of England. Your Birdsong dog is *the* dog. I am the originator of them. First bred them in Virginia twenty-four years ago, from pure parent stock and a judicious system afterwards of selecting and crossing until I am of the opinion they are nearly perfection. I hunted them in Virginia two years, against all comers and never found the first dog that could live with them in a red fox chase and come out alive. The same thing can be said by Mr. Birdsong, to whom I gave the pack twenty-one years ago. I see from the last *"Turf, Field and Farm"* that at the great match race at Oil Springs, held in November last, that "the celebrated Birdsong dogs owned by Mr. H. C. Trigg, of Glasgow, Kentucky, exhibited game and speed." That coming from a Madison man is a compliment. There are no fox hounds anywhere to be found can speed or stay with these dogs. Should I ever visit Kentucky I shall certainly accept your invitation and call and see you.
                              Respectfully yours,
                                   T. Y. HENRY.

————

                        THOMASTON, GA., April 23, 1867.
H. C. Trigg, Esq.,

DEAR SIR: Yours of the 8th inst. duly received and I avail myself of the earliest opportunity of replying. I have selected two of the oldest puppies for you and can send you a very superior young dog three years old for $100. He is throughbred of my full stock, *well broke* and reliable.. A good strike dog, has a good nose and is very rapid and superior trailer, distinguished for taking off a track when lost. His speed among my dogs is only medium, though when running on a moderately high scent it takes a very fast dog to lead him. He seems to run as fast by scent as by sight. He is a dog of great bottom and endurance, a dog of never-tiring energy and perseverance. Indeed he has too much in him. His mouth on a trail is tolerably good and he uses it free enough. When he first scents he will whimper and squeal a few times; after this his mouth is full and tolerably coarse. When running at full speed his mouth is a clear, loud, long shrill note. He is a tall, lean raw-boned dog, and very poor at this time, so much so I dislike to send him to you. His health is good, but he is such a restless, inveterate hunter that I can not keep him in condition on the scant allowance I am compelled to mete out to my dogs during the summer months in these times of famine. He goes to the hunting ground by himself about twice a week and runs an old red fox to his burrow. I have given you a fair description of the dog, George. You will find him as represented. If you want him send me check on New York for the whole amount, $150.

My dogs are thoroughbred *fox-hounds* and pursue the fox as instinctively as a pointer will sit or pause at the scent of his first bird. You will find the puppies I send you to be well broke and reliable on the first drag of a red fox that they scent. If they do not take the first drag or if they quit it to pursue any other kind of game I will refund the money you paid for them. Since you have sent me an order for them I feel free to say more in their praise than I should have done. I never have to break my dogs. All that is necessary is to take them out early on the ground where foxes are. They will soon know all about the habits of the fox. My dogs prefer the scent of the red fox to that of any other game, and a few of them become very indifferent to a gray fox after running a red. I prefer to let my young dogs run rabbits about the farm until they are two years old before entering them for a red fox. They take to it just as readily, and they last much longer by it. I could send you some dogs, crosses on my stock belonging to my friends, for from twenty-five to fifty dollars, but they are aged and second rate. I could not recommend them as red fox dogs, but are good gray fox dogs. You will find that the gray fox will disappear after a while when the reds establish themselves firmly, and you had better prepare in time for them. To become a successful red fox hunter you must divest yourself of all *old-time prejudices.* *Hunting* red foxes and catching red foxes are two things. Any one can hunt them. You can't sit with your leg over the pommel of your saddle and hear your dogs run in a briar thicket for an half hour, and the pack that dwells upon the drag or goes back to take a second scent to assure themselves that the game is about will never be again so near a red fox as they were at the start.

The red fox is a very wild, cowardly animal. He trusts nothing to cunning, but everything to heels. He will get up as far ahead of the hounds as possible and continue to distance his pursuers until he gets far enough ahead to maintain his advantage at his natural gait, which is a long leap. If permitted to pursue his own gait, the d——I couldn't catch him, for he can run a week. To overcome all the advantage in favor always of the pursued, you must have dogs that will push ahead on a faint scent, and make quick and rapid casts ahead on the line of chase and speed enough, with *a good high scent*, to push the fox to his utmost rate of speed, and then if your hounds have got the bottom and endurance to keep him up to his rate he is bound to strike his flag to them in from sixty minutes to two hours. When you have got speed it becomes then a question of endurance; without speed the test can not be applied. I have never seen one of the old-fashioned stag hounds with their deep, mellow, long-toned mouths that had speed to cope with the red fox, and I have learned to love the short chops of the more speedy fox-hounds. It sounds like success, and I had rather glimpse a flying pack at breakneck speed than to sit half a day and listen to the slow drolling notes of a slow pack.

The pleasure of the chase is *not* in the pursuit with me; 'tis the catch at the finale that overflows my cup. Having successfully pursued red foxes for the last twenty years, I venture these remarks to you. Commencing life with a shattered and feeble constitution, I feel indebted to fox hunting for a long lease on life, and hope it may be the means of restoring you to health.

Hoping to hear from you soon, I am

Very respectfully,

G. L. F. BIRDSONG.

P. S. I enclose a letter to show you how my dogs are prized here. I sold Longstreet for $200 in a lot of others. After he was sold, Dr. Sterling, of Lagrange, wrote to buy him. I wrote to Mr. Ward he could sell Longstreet at a profit and here you have his laconic reply, Yours, etc.,

G. L. F. B.

CUTHBERT, GA., March 1, 1867.

To G. L. F. Birdsong, Esq.,

MY DEAR FRIEND. I send you this evening $500. I hope you will receive it.

Tell the gentleman whom you spoke of buying Longstreet that he will never have money enough to buy him from me.

Your friend,

A. G. WARD.

THOMASTON, GA., May 29, 1867.

H. C. Trigg, Esq.,

DEAR SIR: On the 22d inst. I shipped you the three dogs per express, George, Chase and Bee, and I hope they will arrive

in good order. The dog is a deep tan (red), tall, lean, white feet and short tail. The dog and bitch pups are both tans (reds), brother and sister. All four feet white and a few white hairs in end of tail. . . . It is very seldom you can find a very fleet dog on the market, and as that quality is most highly prized they always command very high figures, say from $150 to $200. I wrote you of a chance to obtain one or two *very fleet* dogs, and if you desire I will purchase for you. Yours, etc.
G. L. F. BIRDSONG.

THOMASTON, GA., June 10, 1867.

H. C. Trigg, Esq.,

DEAR SIR: Yours of the 28th of May came to hand on the 3d inst., and I hasten to reply. I am truly sorry the dogs did not come up to your expectations. I endeavored to prepare your mind for their condition. Dogs necessarily fare badly in a country where famine stalks abroad in daylight, and it is strange that thousands of worthless curs are not destroyed by their owners. A great many dogs actually perished to death last summer and it is incredible how long they can endure hunger and starvation. I know of one pack of hounds that subsisted entirely on roasting ears and watermelons as they gathered them from the stalks and vines.

I have written to secure the dog Forest for you, but I very much fear he can not be bought singly at any price. If I can get Forest for $100 I will let you have one of my finest bitches for $100, or the two for $200, as you proposed. I did not think I would part with this bitch, Fannie, but as you are somewhat disappointed with those sent you, and as you feel you are paying a high price for dogs and much more than your friends are paying for fine dogs, I am determined you shall have the *very best* specimens of my stock, and if they do not sustain themselves and their reputation in a contest with the Tennessee dogs it will be the first time they ever failed to do it.

The bitch, Fannie, is three years old, medium in size, a

perfect model of *symmetry* and beauty. She is well worth $200 to any man fond of fine fox-hounds, and you will not take that for her after you get her in your possession. She has been in Jasper county where I have been breeding her. I enclose letter from Mr. Robinson, who bred her for me on shares. He hunted her last winter with his dogs. You must admit that the performance of his dogs are good enough. He hunts with a small pack, only seven dogs, and he caught with them *above* ground, fairly and squarely, twenty red foxes and two gray foxes. His dogs were sired by Boston, the maternal half brother of Fannie. I sold him when fourteen months old for $150. Very respectfully,

GEO. L. F. BIRDSONG.

June 28, 1867.

Mr. G. L. F. Birdsong,

I received your note by your son, Henry. You state you have sold Fannie and your son tells me it is to a gentleman in Kentucky. I am sorry to learn that Fannie is going to leave the country, as I consider her one of the best bitches in the State. In other words, I do not believe there is a better dog living than Fannie. She has all the qualities that constitute a No. 1 red fox dog, both in regard to trailing and running. Some may perhaps be a little faster than Fannie when the fox first gets up, but after running one hour no dog can excel her. I regret not getting some pups from her, as she has not been to a dog since I carried her to July nearly a year ago.

We caught last season twenty red foxes, and caught them all in good time, from one to three hours, and Fannie was at the catching of all of them and sustained herself well. She has made for herself in this county a character as a red fox dog that none can excel. I would like for you to give her a race or two before you send her off, just to see how she does perform after a red fox, and I am sure you will be pleased with her. I will write before long and give you the particulars in regard to our races last season.

Very respectfully,
JOHN L. ROBINSON.

NEWTON COUNTY, GA.

THOMASTON, GA., June 30, 1867.

H. C. Trigg, Esq.,

DEAR SIR: I have only time to say that I secured you two fine dogs and will ship them to you on the 4th of July, without fail. Will write you particulars when I ship them. Bill $200, which you can send me in greenbacks by express, or check as before.
Yours truly,
G. L. F. BIRDSONG.

THOMASTON, GA., July 3, 1867.

H. C. Trigg, Esq.,

DEAR SIR: After writing you a few days since that I had bought two dogs for you, Dora and Wheeler, I sent up after them to ship you, and enclosed you will find a note from Mr. Bradley explaining why the dogs were not shipped. He backed squarely out of it, and you see some of the difficulties in getting my trained dogs even at high figures. I have to-day bought a fine dog, Rip, that is all right. No fault except age; he is five or six years old. I ran him in his first season in my pack when he was about a year old and he sustained himself well with Longstreet; was about the same age, probably a little older. I have now nothing left but to send you Fanny. Mr. Robinson was loth to give her up and offered to buy her himself. He says she is the best bitch for red foxes in the State. He caught twenty last winter and Fanny was at the death of them all. If you want the dog Broxton send me one hundred dollars and I will buy him for you and ship him to you. The price of Fanny and Rip is two hundred dollars, which you can send me. The young dog, Lee, I present to you. He ran last winter a very hard race, after a red fox, after which he became lame in his right hind leg. I think he has fully recovered and will make you a fine dog.

Very respectfully,
Geo. L. F. Birdsong.

Thomaston, Ga., August 26, 1867.

H. C. Trigg, Esq.,

Dear Sir: Your letters of the 12th and 16th inst. came to hand yesterday and I hasten to reply, and will try to post this letter to-morrow so that it will reach you with all possible dispatch. I enclose you a letter from Mr. Ward, of Green county. You will see I have prevailed upon him to let you have Forest. He is out of a bitch I bred and sold to Mr. Ward and is all right in pedigree, and not too nearly related to Fanny. You can see what Mr. Ward says of him. Mr. Ward is a high minded Southern gentleman. He never boasts of dogs or speaks of them in superlative terms; what he says of Forest is as much praise as he ever bestows on his dogs. The bitch Echo to whom he refers is now in my kennel. Mr. Ward tested her fully with Forest, and I have tested her with Longstreet, and I can say that if Forest can be truthfully compared to her, that he is fast enough and good enough for any purpose. She is one of the few dogs I believe able to kill a red fox by herself in from one to two hours. Longstreet has done it several times in less time than that. I shall breed Echo to July when in season which is close at hand, as she whelped last December, and if you wish will try and let you have a pair of the puppies as a special favor, though I have engaged more of July's pups than I can supply this season. I have a litter of five from July and Springfield now a week old, but I think I shall keep them. If you want the dog Forest you had better write or telegraph Mr. Ward immediately. You had better order direct as it will cost me twenty-five dollars to send overland one hundred miles to get him for you. There is no chance to get Wheeler from Mr. Bradley upon any terms. He and Mr. Gorman, of the adjoining county, are very intimate, and if anybody gets Wheeler it will be Mr. Gorman. The red fox came within twelve miles of him and he caught four of them. This winter they will be nearer. Rip is a cross of the blue speckled hound common to this country thirty years ago. He is the third generation from the cross. I think you did right to stint Bee. I always adopt that plan with young bitches unless under some urgent necessity. The best plan is to hunt the bitches; you can then see their defects and their good points, and correct the one and perfect the other by a judicious selection of a dog. Education and habits are to a certain extent transmitted to the offspring, especially by the female, and the imagination exerts some influence during the period of gestation, therefore, I prefer to hunt the bitches during the early period of pregnancy. There is but little risk to run from accident as their muscles during this period become soft and they are incapable of making great exertions. I have known several instances of their being delivered at the natural time during a fox chase.

Very respectfully,
GEO. L. F. BIRDSONG.

———

THOMASTON, July 30, 1867.

H. C. Trigg, Esq.,

DEAR SIR: Yours of the 15th and 16th inst. duly received and would have been answered sooner but for my indisposition. My health continues feeble and am becoming, in consequence, desponding. Two years from now the Birdsong dogs will be in great demand in your State. It has always been so wherever I have sent them, and it is bound to be so with you. They can catch red foxes, and I can send you a pack of letters attesting that fact and dating back from 1854 to the present time, but you have better evidence before you.

You have the dogs that have done it, and can do the trick again as well in Kentucky as in Georgia.

As to my mode of hunting, I do not take my dogs to the field coupled; sometimes I go eight or ten miles to the hunting grounds of a morning. I am too old now to stand so much work and prefer to be much nearer. My dogs run loose and when acquainted with the ground go ahead and frequently have the fox running when I get there. We trail up our foxes fairly, and this is the style in all the Southern States where fox hunting is carried on for sport. I never halloo to or encourage my dogs till the fox is unkenneled, and then only at certain times when a halloo is irresistible. I am a very still, quiet hunter, and you must be so, too, if you want to be successful in catching red foxes. They are very wild and steal off from their kennel before a noisy hunter is within a half a mile of them. If your dogs are well bred they will need no encouragement. Never halloo when you see the fox and your dogs are running or coming to you, it will distract their attention and take them off of their nose, and will probably cause them to lose or at least be at fault for awhile. Sit still and let them pass, and then if they seem tired and you think encouragement is needed or if you *can't help* it, give a few short screams and ride beside them a little way, or all the time if you can. When dogs are some distance from you, say half a mile or more, it does them no good to halloo to them—they don't hear you, but the fox does and quickens his pace. When the dogs are running off I sometimes halloo a peculiar way to inform other hunters which way the dogs are going. We signal on the horn to each other, and I train my dogs to a certain signal when I see a fox and want to get them close after him. When you first unkennel and part of the dogs are about to get off, you must halloo to get the pack together, but never halloo unless you have an object in it. My dogs never quit a fox as long as they can smell him. *Don't hunt with a large pack of strange dogs* in expectation of much sport. From seven to ten dogs is enough to kill a red fox. Hunt them together after gray foxes and rabbits until they get well acquainted with each other. Let them know each other "clean through and through;" have them about the same speed. Feed high and exercise well. Select a good, damp, foggy morning in October or November and be on the ground by daylight (if the fox is wild and steals away before the dogs 'tis best to be on the ground before day); put your dogs as close to the fox as possible and be quiet. If you are acquainted with the country keep with your dogs if possible.

A red fox is like a deer and has a certain line of country to run over. One word as to foxes. Every hunter who fails to catch a fox thinks that fox the toughest one out. I wish you could see my file of letters from huntsmen from different sections of this and the adjoining States, inviting me to come and catch one of their red foxes. They all think my foxes not so good as theirs. I go, and have never yet found any difference. They don't stand before me any longer than those I encounter here.

I wrote a history of the red fox of America, which was published in the "*Countryman,*" 1764. They were imported from England by one of the old English Governors of New York and turned loose on Long Island during a severe winter and they crossed over on the ice to the main land, and have steadily migrated southwesterly along and parallel to the great mountain range of the Middle States. Their progress can be easily traced all along. In 1840, when I got my dogs from Virginia and Maryland, there were no red foxes west of the Conee river, Georgia. They had migrated to the eastern banks of that stream. Since then they have crossed that stream and occupy the country between that stream and the Ocmulgee. Finding in 1840 that the gray foxes were too slow for my dogs, I sent an order to Porter of the "*Spirit of the Times,*" for a pair of red foxes and you will see his reply to G. L. F. B. in the enclosed slip, "To Correspondent." **The first pair the dog fox was caught on Long Island the**

Vixen in the State of New York and she stood up six and a half hours in a soft, heavy snow before she burrowed.

From these sprung a numerous progeny that is now extended from the Flint river west to the Chattahoochee. There is but little difference between these New York foxes and those that have migrated from the East. There are two varieties here. One a small, deep red, pony-built fox, very little white on the tail; the other a light yellow, several inches of the tail being white, sometimes a little white on the toes, long, tall, and very wild. I think these foxes as stout as any and they are certainly in the worst country for dogs to run over I ever saw. If I had money, as "I used to," before this "cruel war," I would mount the train, with three or four couples of my dogs and would be at that big hunt on the 16th of October. I would then and there see "what is what." If you will come down this fall with five or six good ones I will meet you and you will receive true Southern welcome and hospitality, and be at no expense after landing. Were we able we would send you a free ticket through, "bag and baggage."

Thanks to Providence, though we be disfranchised, we will have a bountiful crop this fall. I rejoice that my poor dogs will soon be fed without stint.

If you will refer to *Turf, Field and Farm*, one of the June numbers, you will see a communication headed "Fox-Hounds and Fox Hunting," by Tally Ho. He speaks of the Irish dogs as being the best red fox dogs in Maryland or Virginia. The dogs I send you are descended from these.

As ever yours, etc.,
GEO. L. F. BIRDSONG.

———

THOMASTON, GA., Sept. 3, 1869.

Mr. H. C. Trigg.

DEAR SIR: Your favor of August 23d at hand, and I regret to announce the death of father, he having died August 18th, after a confinement of seven weeks. He died with

JAKE. HENDOO—ELLA.

consumption. Also regret to hear you have lost Delta and Lightfoot, but you ought to be able to catch red foxes with your pack this fall. Would like so much to see them run, Madcap is dead, old July is doing well, Echo is with pup by July also four others, so we can not have any sport before December. July is getting too old to run, only fit for breeding purposes. I am glad to hear you think so much of Chase; we have his brother and he is hard to outrun. I think your two pups from King and Delta will not prove anything extra, judging from what I have heard of Mr. Waddy's dog, King, but hope they may prove extra. You have no pups from Delta and Lightfoot, have you? That was my choice to breed from. I will be glad to hear from you occasionally and the performance of your pack this fall.

As ever your friend,
GEO. P. BIRDSONG.

Being called on by my friend, neighbor and fellow huntsman John S. Jackson, for the pedigree of his fast running dog Jane whose fleetness I am well acquainted with (as well as many others). Jane was sired by my dog July about the year 1861. I brought July from Maryland. His sire was imported from Ireland, and known as the "Irish Red Foxhound." . . . . I have been a constant fox hunter for the last forty years and have tried all kinds of dogs, but could never catch more than one fox out of every ten chases until I introduced the Irish dogs. Since then I catch at least seven out of every ten. Believing the Irish stock to be the finest in the world I do hereby subscribe myself

MILES G. HARRIS.

JULY 22, 1868.

GREEN COUNTY, GA., Oct. 3, 1867.

DEAR SIR: Your favor of the 17th ult. has been received. Also received by express $100 for Forest. Please accept my thanks for the prompt remittance. Forest is out of Reel, a slut presented to me by Mr. Birdsong when a pup. She was one-half or three-quarters Irish, with, I think, a cross upon the Maryland dogs introduced by him into this State. His sire, Boston, was out of a half Irish slut; grandsire Willis, was from a Virginia dog and slut. Boston is still living, and has been a remarkable fox-hound. Willis was also a very superior dog. Reel and Boston's mother were excellent dogs. Forest has a sister in this county of the same age of himself that is prized very highly by her owner, he having refused $100 for her last winter. Forest is yours now, and if you will recruit and manage him properly he will prove what I believe him to be, one of the finest red fox-hounds I ever knew.

I notice in the *Turf, Field and Farm* that you have spirited fox hunters in Madison and other counties in your State. Would it be inconvenient for you to enter Forest for the horn they propose to be run for in November? I have thought that Forest acquitted himself better with a strange pack than when running with my own as though he considered the honor greater to beat them. It would afford me much pleasure to know he had won for his spirited owner so fine a trophy as the champion horn of Kentucky.

Very respectfully,

R. H. WARD.

P. S.—The name of Boston's mother I can't recall just now. She belonged to a neighbor and was of Irish and Redbone stock. I gave her to him when a pup.

GREEN COUNTY, GA., June 16, 1868.

H. C. Trigg, Esq.,

DEAR SIR: Your favor was received a few days since. I have felt disappointed at you not writing to me earlier, especially at your not acknowledging the receipt of the puppy sent you. In regard to Echo, my nephew has sold her to a gentleman living near Mr. Birdsong for $150, and I rather suspect for Mr. B. himself. She is a very superior hound. You have Lightfoot her full brother; take care of him for I consider him an excellent dog and there is no better stock in Georgia. He resembles his sire more than any of his get I have ever seen. Their sire July was procured from Gosnell, of Maryland. They had many good qualities and among them this, that after running an hour or two or longer they are as quick and press forward with as much eagerness as in the outset. Mr. Birdsong's Irish were remarkable dogs.

Very respectfully,

R. H. WARD.

GREEN COUNTY, GA., Sept. 7, 1868.

H C. Trigg.

DEAR SIR: I will in a day or two ship by express to you three hounds, Hampton, Rose, and Emma Sampson, the latter named for the girl that piloted General Forrest across the river when in pursuit of the Federals. If Hampton had the loins of Forest he would be perfect in form. Please take good care of him and not allow him to serve many sluts, as excessive service is very injurious, one *coition* being quite enough. I never bred a dog that I thought so much of. He is a natural fox-hound.

Rose is one year older than Hampton, full sister to Echo and Lightfoot (by July), and is highly prized by Captain Brown. You will be pleased with her. Emma is a full sister to Hampton and possesses more speed than either Hampton or Rose. All three are from my old Flora. I should be glad to get a pair of puppies from Hampton and the slut General Maupin gave you.

Very respectfully your friend,

R. H. WARD.

P. S.—Rose is black, the other two red.

GREEN COUNTY, GA., Oct. 21, 1868.

H. C. Trigg.

DEAR SIR: I was very much gratified at the flattering account you gave of Forest's performance in your last letter. He is the first and only dog I ever sold and were my circumstances such as they were before the war five times the amount you gave me would not have bought him. As it is I am perfectly satisfied, he is now owned by a gentleman who knows his value as a fox hound and fully appreciates it. Now as to Hampton. Before his injury, for a ten to twenty hour chase I don't believe his equal could be found. He would roam the fields like a pointer, performing twice the labor of any other dog. And it would have required tendons of steel to have sustained him. Rose, you will find without making much ado about it, a steady, reliable dog of stoutness and courage. Emma has speed and I hope when she becomes familiar with your pack will give you some evidence of it. Delta I have heard of before you got her, as being a very fine fox-hound of speed about equal to her mother, Echo. . . . I imagine that your pack when in full cry, if they do not touch chords of sweetest sound, would at least make such a maddening fuss at to wake up the echoes of the vale and pester the lifeless soul that never knew the bewitching enchantment of sweet melody.

I need not tell you I shall be glad to her from you at any time. Your friend,

R. H. WARD.

GREEN COUNTY, GA., Nov. 10, 1868.

H. C. Trigg.

DEAR SIR: Your favor of the 4th inst. was received today and I hasten to reply. Let me beg you to entertain no unpleasant reflections in reference to Hampton's death. It was one of those unavoidable misfortunes that no precaution could have prevented, so don't allow it to disturb you the least in the world. You ask me what compensation you shall give me for him. Nothing under the sun. I should consider myself unworthy the respect of an honorable huntsman were I to receive a single cent for him. Dismiss all idea of compensation. I never intended selling Hampton to you. My object in sending him to you was for you to keep him during this hunting season and longer if you desired, and then present him to a friend in Southern Georgia, who had honored me by naming his son for me.

I desire a pair of Rose's puppies for him. I fear you will have other cases of hydrophobia in your kennels. I should very much regret to learn that your fine pack had been broken up by it, especially as you have incurred such heavy expense and been at so much trouble in collecting them.

Your friend,
R. H. WARD.

CLAY VILLAGE, KY., May 12, 1870.

Mr. U. C. Trigg.

DEAR SIR: I have deferred writing longer than I intended. When you sent Tip up I received a letter from you saying that your young dogs had beaten mine, which was exactly what I expected. I told Ford and Howell the day we were out that if we got a race your dogs would beat us, but Howell said until that was done he would not believe it. Perhaps you will think it strange when I say that if my dogs proved to be faster than yours I would be sorry for it, but nevertheless it is so, because I am, and have been for years, looking for dogs that could beat mine, and yours are decidedly the fastest I have found.

I want you to test Waxie thoroughly with yours and if he proves to be faster than yours we will have to import a pair. Out of your next litter please save me a full brother to the two you had up here. Ford told me while I was speaking to speak for him; he wants one. Venus lost her pups, and Josephine only had two, both sluts. If you want one of them write me.

Yours with respect,
W. L. WADDY.

CLAY VILLAGE, KY., Dec. 5, 1870.
H. C. Trigg,
 DEAR SIR: I received your very welcome letter of Nov. 29th and read it with interest. Mr. Ford informs me he had two races since his return. He says Forest (by your old Forest) came to the hole six hundred yards ahead of the pack. I am now thoroughly satisfied a cross with Forest (the old dog) and Venus, and King and Delta bred together, their produce can not be beaten in the United States. Breed Money to a pup of Venus and Echo to Forest, which is just the same cross. Have you been fortunate enough to hear anything of your lost dogs? Remember me to your amiable lady. Most respectfully your friend,
W. L. WADDY.

CLAY VILLAGE, KY., July 18, 1872.
Friend Trigg,
 I have neglected writing to you so long I am ashamed of such negligence, but hope you will pardon me. . . . . . There is nothing in the dog line I regret so much as the loss of your old Forest The litter of pups of Echo and Forest I was looking to as going to be the best litter of pups in Kentucky. My last hunt has satisfied me that Echo is worth all the dogs I have. She is running as far ahead of my dogs as ever King did. When Delta will run she is the only one of my dogs that can keep in hearing of her. The pup you sent me has had the mange, but I think will make a great dog when he gets well. Echo's pups by young Forest are very promising. They show great game and speed. My respects to your good lady.
W. L. WADDY.

CLAY VILLAGE, KY., June 8th.
H. C. Trigg.
 DEAR SIR: I received your letter a few days ago; was glad

foxes on the ground a few days since. The ring-necked pup you sent me has gotten well at last and is running in the lead of the pack a good part of the time, etc.

Yours,

W. L. WADDY.

RICHMOND, KY., April 6, 1869.

H. C. Trigg, Glasgow, Ky.:

DEAR SIR: Your favor has been duly received. In reply to your query about the pups I gave you, I think I may safely assert that there is not anywhere a better bred dog. Her blood is unexceptionable. I will now give you her pedigree and something of her ancestry. She was out of my brother Will's Crickette and was by Warren Harris' Pete (better known as Blind Pete); Crickette was out of Maggie and was by David Irvin's Boston; Maggie was out of Joe Shackelford's Vic and was by Dr. Jake White's Duke; Shackelford's Vic was out of my father's old Vic and was by his English dog Fox; old Vic was out of W. R. Fleming's old Nan and was got by his dog Bascom; Nan and Bascom both came from Maryland and were of the purest stock; Irvin's Boston was brought from South Carolina by Add White. He was certainly purely bred, fast, and fine. He was a splendid deer dog. Duke was out of Jake White's Queen and was by his dog Collier; Queen was out of J. M. White's Lal, and was by old Rifle (a dog imported from England by my father in 1857, very fine and fast); Lal was out of Martin Gentry's Ellen and was by General Maupin's famous dog Lead; Ellen was out of Gentry's Cry and by his dog Money (both came from Virginia); Fox was out of old Queen (imported by my father from England in 1857) and was got by Rifle. He was a full brother to Jeff Maupin's Bragg, Durrett's White's Bally, and others, amongst the best ever raised here or elsewhere. White's Collier was a Virginia dog, fine, fast, and good. Maupin's Lead came from Governor Nelson's in East Tennessee, was very fast and was regarded by General Maupin as the best dog he ever owned.

Ellen and Duke (her full brother) were two of the fastest dogs I ever saw. Duke I regarded as the best hunter, the fastest, and altogether the best dog I ever saw. My father's Vic was the fastest dog after a deer in America. I believe she was a good fox dog. She was the mother of Fitz, Mac, Doe, and many other fast and good ones. She was half sister to our old Florence. Blind Pete was out of Kavanaugh's Blonde and by Jeff Maupin's Bragg (full brother to Fox and Bally and others); Blonde was out of John Moberley's old red bitch and was by General Maupin's Lead (the Tennessee dog); Moberley's bitch was out of a very fine and fast bitch brought here from Virginia and was got by Jeff Maupin's Buck, who also came from Virginia. Blonde was the mother of Jeff Maupin's Drum the "Red Dog." (this was Kavanaugh's dog) Pete, and Upas, all the finest and fastest kind.

Your pup combines the blood of all the finest, fastest and best dogs that we ever had in this country. I do not see how she can be otherwise than good and fast. You may hunt the world over and you will not find a better bred stock dog. I think she will nick exactly with your Birdsong dogs. Until recently the boys have not hunted much since General Maupin's death. They have, however, begun to revive the sport again. Your friend,

C. J. WALKER.

LOUISVILLE, KY., September 1, 1873.

H. C. Trigg, Esq.,

DEAR SIR: Your favor of 28th came duly to hand and about ten minutes after receiving it the express wagon drove up with the pups, for which I am under many obligations. They were received in good order and I immediately expressed them to Alex Fible in Oldham county. I intended to give them to my cousin in Bullitt county, but Fible heard I was going to get them and was so anxious to have them, and as I go up there a great deal I let him have them. I like their looks very much and am satisfied they will make good ones. Thanking you again for the pups, I am yours truly,

C. B. SIMMONS.

These puppies were by Chase. He by Longstreet. They were out of Annie, she out of Rose and Rose was by old July. These puppies as dogs made a great reputation. Their produce and descendants are owned to-day and highly prized in the counties of Jefferson, Henry, and Bullitt.

——— H. C. TRIGG.

KINGSTON, KY., July 11, 1870.

H. C. Trigg,

DEAR SIR: I was requested several days ago by George to write and inform you he had been sick. He has received your letter. We have tried Minnie; she is a good runner. George is willing for you to have her at $100 if you still wish her as you seem to be so much attached to her. He can buy a dog here that will suit him as well. He says there is no other living man could buy her for love or money. He is very low to-day, suffering greatly. He keeps Minnie in his room all the time. I remain

Respectfully,
SETH W. MAUPIN.

KINGSTON, KY., Feb. 1, 1871.

H. C. Trigg,

DEAR FRIEND: As I had not heard whether you received Minnie or not, I thought I would drop you a few lines inquiring if you had received her. I shipped by Adams Express some three weeks ago. I have been uneasy about her by you not writing back. I would like very much to see you and Lightfoot and Cricket up here. I dare you to come. Red foxes are all over the country now, and run well. I think Towstring can beat you. Write and let me know when you can come. Your friend,

GEO. W. MAUPIN.

KINGSTON, KY., July 25, 1870.

Mr. Trigg.

I received your note, dated the 19th. You want to know if I would sell Towstring, and my price on him. I have had bad luck since you were up here—lost my wife and had my house burned—and can not hunt a great deal. My price for Towstring is one hundred dollars. You wish to know what Towstring could do. I think he can beat any dog in the State. In a word, he is the best red fox dog I ever saw, understands them better and is always willing to do his part. He will go farther to start a fox than any dog I ever saw. Write full directions how you want him sent. I ran him after a deer. He lost every dog and caught the deer in two hours. I hope I can come down this fall.

JEFF. MAUPIN.

SCOOBA, MISS., April 24, 1890.

Mr. Haiden Trigg, Glasgow, Ky.,

DEAR SIR: Some years ago my friend, R. G. Caldwell, formerly of your city, shipped me a hound from your pack named Chase. He proved to be a very fine dog, I think the best I ever owned. We crossed him with a good bitch and raised some fine hounds, but not to be compared with the old dog. I am very anxious to get a pair of pups from your best dogs. Please let me know if you can let me have them, and what price. An early reply will greatly oblige.

Yours truly,

H. M. DUKE.

This dog was bred in my kennel and was full Birdsong.

GRENADA, MISS., Dec. 17, 1892.

Col. H. C. Trigg.

MY DEAR SIR: I bought Ann and last year her pup, Houston, from Mr. W. S. Walker. I have Ann now. I ran Houston to death. He was the best dog I ever saw. Mr. Walker, of Garrard county, Ky., from whom I got them, wrote me that your dog, Houston, was his sire. I want to know if I can get either his sire, Houston, or some well bred dog from you. I think the Birdsong dogs "X" on my Walker bitches would make extra dogs. If you can spare me one give age, size, color and breeding.

Yours truly,
J. J. SLACK.

BOWLING GREEN, KY., Dec. 31, 1894.

W. L. Porter.

DEAR SIR: Answering your inquiry as to my opinion of the "Trigg dogs," I will say that I have known this stock of dogs for twenty years or more, and I believe them to be the best dogs for red foxes in the State of Kentucky.

Respectfully,
BEN F. GARDNER,
Treasurer B. G. Kennel Club.

BOWLING GREEN, KY., Dec. 21, 1894.

Fenton Hagerman, Esq.,

DEAR HAGERMAN: I learn from a private letter that it will soon be possible to obtain some dogs from the celebrated Trigg Kennel, and advise that you go there to further build up the pack. I have known these dogs for twenty years and have no hesitation in saying that as red fox dogs they have no equals in this State, and I have known most of the leading kennels, have hunted with them and have owned some good dogs myself. The care which has always been used in mating, in training and working them, added to an original pure pedigree, has enabled these dogs to earn that distinction. The Hodo of Uncle Remus' story in *Scribner* could have made nothing off of Forest, Baby, Chase, Money or Wildgoose in a twenty mile "sail to winward and return" with a well groomed dog fox at the front. In my opinion they are the best dogs in Kentucky, and sometimes even in our rough

country they kill their quarry fairly in the open. We bred our best Kennel Club bitches to Steve and Don of this pack and next season we can show you some swift and courageous dogs. Your friend,
WILLIAM L. DULANEY.

BOWLING GREEN, KY., Dec. 20, 1894.
J. M. Brents, Esq.,

DEAR SIR: We have bred our best bitches to some of the dogs in the kennel of H. C. Trigg, Esq., and value the produce more highly than any other young things we have. The dogs and bitches which we own and which came from the same kennel are most excellent red fox dogs, and we think one of the bitches, the celebrated Merideth slut, the best red fox dog in the world. This is the opinion of all our members.
W. S. OVERSTREET,
President Bowling Green Kennel.

BURKSVILLE, KY., Jan. 13, 1895.
H. C. Trigg,

DEAR SIR: In reply to yours of recent date in regard to the bitch I sent you, her name is Annie. She has had two litters of pups neither by curs. The most of her offspring is in this comitry. They are all fine runners, though not by a thoroughbred dog. As for speed and endurance, my experience is that they can not be excelled anywhere, and I have had an experience of twenty years running fox-hounds. I would not have any other stock of dogs. Send me two choice puppies and let me hear how you are pleased with Annie.
Yours truly,
J. C. HERRIFORD.

WEATHERFORD, TEXAS, Jan. 15, 1895.
Col. H. C. Trigg,

DEAR SIR AND FRIEND: Yours of — date received asking my opinion of the Trigg dogs.

Well, I hardly know what to say, as I feel that I can

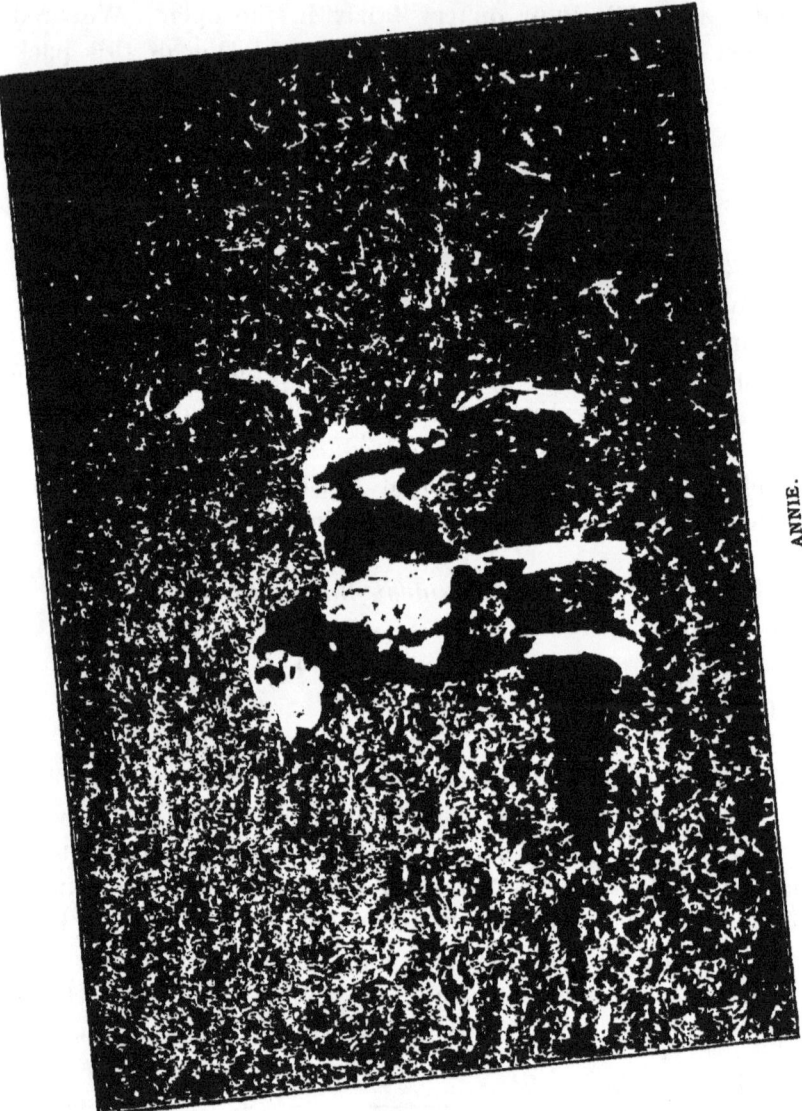

ANNIE.
Houston — Rachel.

hardly say enough for the fine qualities of these dogs. They excel any dogs I ever knew, although I commenced to ride to hounds fifty years ago. They excel in nose, mouth, speed and endurance, and are the most sensible hounds living, being easy trained for the game you want and if petted will come any reasonable distance to their master. We sometimes have long stretches after wolves. Sometimes they escape after deer and he has to be eaten alive or get to deep water, but they always return to their master, either at home or in camp. Yours truly,

J. R. COUTS.

We have met noted packs on different occasions, once on a wager, and we have always beaten them badly with the Trigg dogs and they have wanted some of our dogs.

J. R. C.

WEATHERFORD, TEXAS, Jan. 5, 1895.

H. C. Trigg.

DEAR SIR: Yours of the 2d to hand and noted, and I would say in regard to your strain of fox-hounds I think they are the fastest and best that I have ever seen. I had two of them in Kentucky and I ran them with all of the best dogs in my county and they never failed to lead the pack and stay to the finish. Since I came to Texas I have seen them on open prairie beat the famous ------- dogs, from East Texas, in a sight race after a wolf; in fact, I have never seen them tested with other dogs that they did not come out ahead.

Your friend,

W. J. MORTON.

P. S. I will see friend Cullum and advise him to take the bitch that you spoke of, for I think it is the best and quickest way to recruit his pack. W. J. M.

WEATHERFORD, TEXAS, Jan. 1, 1895.

H. C. Trigg,

DEAR SIR: I have just returned from a deer hunt and found your letter awaiting me, and was glad to hear from you as I have often wanted to correspond about your dogs for I think they are the fastest in the South. The little bitch, Maud, I have is the fastest dog I ever saw and is a stayer. Her breeding is as Mr. Couts wrote. You spoke of the last dog you sold the boys at Weatherford, Jim. I run him and he was a grand dog. He is dead now; a wolf killed him up at Mineral Wells, about twenty-five miles from Weatherford. Write me what is your fastest dog and your price on him. Will be glad to hear from you.

Very truly,

C. M. MILLER.

LOUISVILLE, KY., Jan. 1, 1895.

H. C. Trigg, Glasgow, Ky.

DEAR SIR: I have since early life indulged more or less in the chase; have owned dogs the greater part of my life. For many years have hunted with what is known as the "Birdsong-Trigg Fox-hound." Some twenty years ago Mr. Trigg presented me with a pair of puppies. The following year he presented a friend of mine, John Shanklin, of Jefferson county, also, with a pair. These dogs we ran for years, and for speed, nose, ranging qualities and dead game excelled any dogs I ever knew. I have hunted with a great many breeds of fox-hounds, but have never known or seen anything equal to these dogs. I have sent their produce to friends in different parts of the country—quite a number to the State of Arkansas—and reports from all parties who received them is that they are superior to any dogs they have ever known. I am glad to hear that the lovers of the chase will have an opportunity to secure these, in my judgment, the best red fox dogs in America. I predict that their already deserved great reputation will be greatly increased, and that no strain

H. C. TRIGG'S RESIDENCE.

of dogs will be regarded so highly as these by those fortunate enough to secure them. Truly yours,
R. C. SNODDY.

BOWLING GREEN, KY., Dec., 4, 1895.

To Whom It May Concern,

Having spent the greater portion of my life in the field, I am authoritatively persuaded to think that I have a right to speak on the question of fox-hounds.

I have had occasion to observe many packs in and out of the chase both as regards breed and "stick-to-it-iveness" and frankly admit that the hounds known as the "Trigg dogs" are superior in all points of excellence to any others which have come under my observation. Their endurance in a word is simply everlasting. Respectfully,
PETER STRANGE (Colored),
Keeper Bowling Green, Ky., Club.

MERIDIAN, MISS., June 1, 1894.

Mr. H. C. Trigg, Glasgow, Ky.,

MY DEAR SIR: Your letter received and read with pleasure. I am satisfied the dogs you had in the sixties were bettr than anything we have now. You are supported in this by such men as Kamp, Ridley and W. H. Luttrell, the oldest hunters in the State of Georgia. Captain Ridley says the fastest dog he ever saw was Mr. Birdsong's Hodo. The Maupin dog I was not so familiar with as he was bred in Kentucky. But the Walker dogs get all of their good traits from this strain, which was composed equally of English and Kentucky blood. Major Crump has promised me a duplicate of a Longstreet chart made out by Birdsong himself. So you can look out for it. Major Crump is having the best July with their pedigrees published, so every Georgian can see the blood of the *Georgia dogs*. I am awaiting this publication with much interest. I am glad to hear you still have the Birdsong-Maupin dog. I wish you could run down and see me and talk over dogs and the chase. With best wishes for your continued good health, I am your friend,

G. V. YOUNG.

POINT LEAVELL, June 17, 1890.

H. C. Trigg,

DEAR SIR: I was at the office this morning when your letter came and I mailed you a postal that I would send Trooper to you in the morning. I will give you some of his breeding and the kind of dog I consider him. He will be three years old next August, by Scott, the toughest and gamest dog I think I ever owned. Out of Lill, Scott by Mack, he by Larrimore's Tupey, he by Maupin's Fitz, he by Tennessee Lead, Scott out of Fannie. She by Richardson's Tickler, he by Maupin's Tickler, Lill by Dash, he by Burk's Tom (one of the best red fox dogs I ever knew), Lill out of Kate, she by Jerry, he by Fox, the full blood English dog owned by Maupin and the sire of Dock and Tickler. Lill died a few months ago. She was twelve years old and I never knew her to pull out of a race, no matter how long it was, in her life; even after she got so old she could not keep up she would stay after the dogs all night the longest and darkest night in the year. I know you know some of these dogs by reputation and I don't believe there is hardly such a bred dog in this part of the State. Now as to what kind of a fox dog he is: He is as fast as I care for; that is, he will contend for the track from the start to finish with any dogs he has ever met, and as fair as a dog can be. He straddles the track and gives mouth free and after he runs three or four hours no dog can beat him giving mouth and few dogs I have ever seen can keep the track from him. He has a fine mouth, short, coarse and fast, and the longer the race the freer he yelps. He trails well, though he don't open as free as some dogs. Will not cry a track twice in the same place, and the best broke dog I ever hunted. I have been hunting him since he was nine months old and never knew him thrown

NATIONAL MEET, YEAR 1892, AT BOWLING GREEN, KY.

out of a race. The only weak point about him is he is not as good a hunter as I would like him to be. You will have to be very careful with him, as he has never had but one home, and the most particular dog I ever saw about who he follows, though he is very friendly with every one he comes about. I hunt almost altogether at night, but I believe almost every one else has quit night hunting. I would not give one race of four or five hours at night for a week's running in day time. I will run Trooper to-night and ship him to you in the morning.

Give me something of the history of the Birdsong dogs. I never saw but one and was not pleased with it. Hoping to hear from you soon, I remain   Yours, etc.,
W. S. WALKER.

WEATHERFORD, TEXAS, Jan. 16, 1895.

H. C. Trigg,

DEAR SIR: You ask for my opinion in regard to your breed of fox-hounds as compared with other fox-hounds. Well, I have been running your dogs for the last four or five years, have run them after fox, wolf, deer and wildcat, and have run with the best dogs in my country and will say that the Trigg dogs were always in the lead and stayed to the finish. They have good nose and mouth and are good game when they catch a wolf. In fact, I regard them the best dogs in the world. And in regard to Jim, the dog we got from you, I think he was the best dog that ever went into the woods. One fall and winter he caught, that I got, twenty-three foxes, seventeen wolves, three deer, and one cat, the best record I ever knew a dog to have. Your friends,

D. CULLUM,
W. J. MORTON.

LOUISVILLE, KY., Feb. 20, 1895.

Mr. H. C. Trigg,

DEAR SIR: I have bred a great many Birdsong-Trigg dogs, and they have proved to be as good if not better than any fox dogs I ever owned. I have been hunting for thirty years and tried to get the best dogs in the country, and I am satisfied that these dogs are equal to any in the land.

Very respectfully,

JACK D. BARBOUR.

TRENTON, KY., Jan. 14, 1895.

DEAR TRIGG: Was glad to hear from you once more. About my pups you gave me, there never was any dogs in this county superior to the dog pup and few could equal Lucy. I named the dog after you and you can bet he was always in front. Old Lucy has raised more fine running dogs, I expect, than any bitch in this end of the State. Write to J. C. Russell, Allensville, and J. S. Standard, of Elkton, about them. J. C. Russell ran Brents and Lucy for several years, and would bet his farm, which was a good one, on them losing anybody's pack.

Your friend,

J. P. RUSSELL.

DEATH OF HORNET.

The following account of the tragic death of Hornet was printed in the *Bowling Green Democrat:* The Kennel Club of the city was invited by that hospitable gentleman, C. C. Smith, Esq., to take an early supper with him on the Friday before Christmas, and, afterward, to match its best dogs against the best of the packs of Ewing Isbell, Esq., and Major Nat Mercer. The invitation was accepted, and Captain Overstreet, Judge Hines, Robert Rodes, Jr., and Fent Hagerman took the dogs of the club, under charge of Kennel Keeper Peter Strange, and went out. The son of Trigg-Nora was at the head of the pack. The club borrowed the dog from Mr. H. C. Trigg some months ago, and a better hound never cried a trail.

After a good supper, horses were mounted and horns sounded and the hunt began. Near Brad Hill's the trail of a red fox was struck. Hornet, as usual, being the first to cry it. It lay breast high, and the twenty-one dogs were soon running as for a man's life. After a spin of two or three miles the chase swerved to the right and struck the railroad near Merritt's crossing. None of the hunters was very close, but the lead at this point was claimed for Isbell's Swet, Major, Major Mercer's Kate, and by the clubmen for old Hornet. Whatever may have been the real truth, it was afterwards remarked that the bugle-like notes of the old dog never seemed clearer or more musical than they did that night as they died out in the far west. The moon shone bright, and for an hour and a half all was still, when on the horizon in the southwest the pack could be heard coming back. Nearer and nearer they came and straight as an arrow. There was no doubt now as to the leadership, for the clear notes of the old dog were almost triumphant in their ring, while the other dogs were bunched but little in the rear. In a moment after the rumble of the evening passenger train drowned the cry of the dogs as it rushed toward the point at which the hunted fox was evidently trying to cross. It seemed to reach this point just ahead of the pack of pursuing dogs. And so it did, but Hornet, who was pressing his quarry, struck the road bed just as the locomotive did. The roar of the train and the glare of its lights did not cause him to hesitate or blanch for one moment and as he sprang eagerly forward with exultant yell the pilot struck him. Presumably he never felt the pain of it, and there he died just as he probably would have wished, pushing a red fox at the head of as good a pack of dogs as there is in Southern Kentucky. It was soon evident, after the train passed, that something was wrong. Hornet's voice was still. In the cave on the old Len Arnold place, a straight mile away, the fox went to earth and quest was made for Hornet. He was found by the roadside, near the point where he was stricken, cold in death. The club had him buried and above him is this inscription:

"He was faithful unto death."

At the regular meeting on Saturday night the horn of the club was ordered to be draped in mourning for one moon in memory of him and this resolution adopted, a copy of which the secretary was directed to transmit to Mr. Trigg under its seal:

"Resolved, That it is with profound regret that we are compelled to communicate to Mr. H. C. Trigg, his owner, the death of Hornet, than whom a more honest, courageous and capable red fox dog has not been known to us. We regret only that his very virtues were the cause of his death, but it is some consolation to know that he died as he had lived, when hunting, 'at the head of the procession.'"

BUYING AND SELLING.

"No animal that lives is more worthless than a worthless hound. I have seen many dear at one dollar per hundred. One hundred dollars is a moderate figure for a good hound."

I sympathize with the new beginners in their efforts to get up a pack of first-class fox-hounds. Many imagine that they can, by purchase, get together a pack of dogs in a month or two that will be able to kill the red fox. We say to our young friends, banish all such thoughts. In the first place you must understand hunting in order to teach your pack— the dogs can't teach you. After you thoroughly master the science, which will require some years, you will be prepared to train your dogs. The surest way to get together a first-rate pack of dogs is to breed, raise and train them yourself. The sporting papers are filled with advertisements offering for sale fox-hounds that are recommended as possessing qualities of first-class dogs, i. e., fine rangers, splendid trailers and dead game. Some of these advertisers may have such animals and are honest in their statements, while others known nothing about hunting, are unreliable and their object is to get money without any consideration. The question presents itself. How is a buyer to be protected? In the first place, you must not be impatient or in too great a hurry to purchase dogs from strangers. You can learn a great deal of such men by exchanging two or three letters. Ask them these questions:

Do you live in the country or city?

What kind of game do you hunt, deer, wolf, red or gray foxes?

How long have you been a hunter?

From whom did you get your stock dogs?

To whom have you sold dogs?

Is the country you hunt over cavernous, i. e., are the holes numerous that the foxes go in when pressed?

How many red foxes have you ever caught?

You can form a very correct opinion by having these questions answered.

Never buy a dog from a man who is not a practical hunter. Beware of men who live in cities and offer for sale half a dozen different breeds of dogs. If the party writes that he has caught a great many red foxes in a season when you know his country is filled with safe burrows and holes, let him keep his fast dogs; they are too fast. You might get the party to get recommendations from known reliable men. If the dealer is honest and truly represents his dogs, you assure him that you are a man of integrity and he will not hesitate to send you a dog on trial, you guaranteeing to pay his price or return the animal in good condition.

The loss in purchase and sale does not always fall on the buyer. I have heard of parties refusing to pay for first-class dogs; in fact trying to swindle the seller. When the seller doubts the integrity of the buyer we would suggest that he be required to give such recommendations by some of his public officials as will insure him to be a gentleman, or have him deposit price of purchase in the nearest bank subject to inspection of dog.

We have sold very few dogs and were fortunate enough in all of our transactions to have gentlemen to deal with, and can say the same in all of our numerous purchases in the last thirty years.

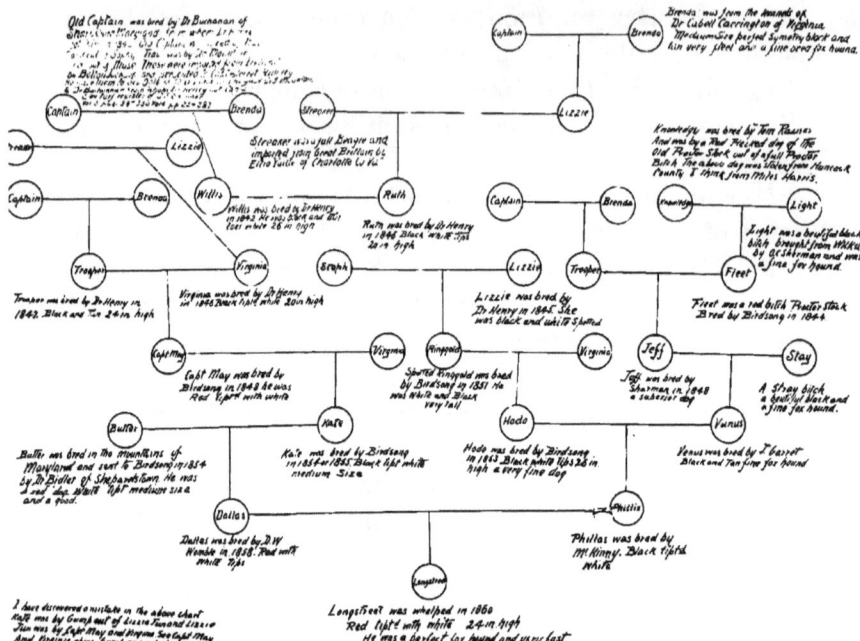

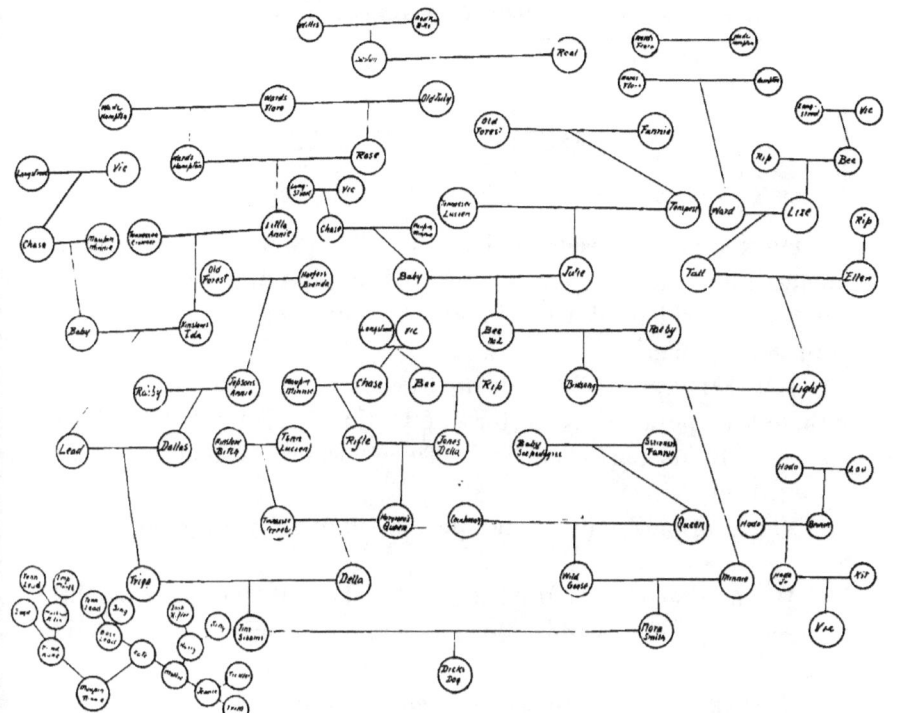

DESCRIPTION OF DOGS.

Dick's Dog.—Bred by Dick Smith, whelped in 1887, 22 inches high, large black and tan, white tips and white breast, ring neck, splendid ranger, fine trailer, dog of great speed and dead game.

Jim Sibbins.—Whelped in 1884, medium size black and tan, white points (see letters of Cullam, Morton, and Miller as regards his performance in Texas, where he made a great reputation).

Nora.—Black and white spotted, fine fox dog, good breeder.

Wild Goose.—Medium size, black and white, splendid ranger, superior trailer, good tongue, celebrated as a start dog.

Minnie.—Black and white, medium size.

Couchman.—From Maupin kennel, white and lemon spots; a dog of great speed.

Queen.—Red or tan, white points, noted for speed.

Baby.—Tan, slightly black on back, prominent white points, ring neck, 24 inches high, powerfully built, noted for great speed and endurance; considered the finest dog of his day.

Scrivner's Waxie.—Old stock, magnificent gray fox dog; noted for ranging qualities, fine trailer and runner.

Birdsong.—Was a very large black and tan.

Light.—Bred and owned by A. Childress; a good fox dog.

Tall.—Bred and raised by Harv. Johnson; black dog with white points.

Rip.—Bred by George L. F. Birdsong, fawn colored, dog of very great energy and speed.

Ward.—Was sent to me when a puppy by Colonel Ward, of Green county, Georgia; black, white points, fine fox dog.

LIZE.—Fawn color, good size, great speed, bred by Dr. Jesse Smith.

BEE.—Bred by George L. F. Birdsong, red or tan, white points, superior speed, dead game.

VIC.—Bred by Joe White, was a fine dog.

LONGSTREET.—Bred by George L. F. Birdsong, whelped in 1860, thought by Mr. B. to be the fastest dog he ever owned, was one of the few dogs that could kill a red fox unaided. See chart.

WARD'S FLORA.—Owned by Colonel R. H. Ward, Green county, Georgia, was a full bred Birdsong and a noted dam, a fine dog.

HAMPTON.—A beautiful red or tan with white points, loaned me by Colonel R. H. Ward, and died in my kennel. See letter regarding his superior qualities.

WADE HAMPTON.—Was presented to Colonel Ward by Wade Hampton, of South Carolina.

RAIBY.—Was from the kennel of Colonel Maupin, white with black and tan spots, strongly built, of great speed and endurance. The best Maupin dog, "Minnie" excepted, ever in my kennel.

BEE No. 2.—Medium size, black and tan, a splendid red fox dog.

JULIA.—A black and tan noted for her ranging and trailing qualities, was a fine dog.

TEMPEST.—Medium size black and tan, owned by Dr. Jesse Smith.

TENNESSEE LUCIAN.—Imported from Tennessee by Seth Kinslow; was a very fine dog.

OLD FOREST.—Black and tan, bred and raised by Colonel R. H. Ward, of Georgia. Secured when four years old. A magnificent red fox dog. Could and did catch red foxes alone and unaided.

FANNIE.—Fawn color, medium size, bred by Mr. Birdsong, a beautiful animal with symmetry of a greyhound. See letter of Mr. Robinson's.

REEL.—Presented to Colonel Ward by Mr. Birdsong, three-fourths Irish, one-fourth "Maryland;" a very excellent fox hound.

BOSTON.—Owned by Colonel Ward and a noted sire of fine fox hounds.

WILLIS.—Was out of a Virginia dog and slut, and a very superior animal.

DELLA.—Was dark fawn in color. Owned by Melvin Lowry, who got her when a puppy from Mr. W. F. Trigg.

GREELEY.—Medium size, black and tan a game fox dog.

HARGROVE'S QUEEN.—Light red, a good dog.

RIELE.—Black and tan, white points, a splendid ranger, fine trailer and dead game.

JONES' DELLA.—Pale red, fine size, with great speed and endurance.

CHASE.—Whelped in 1865, purchased with Bee from Mr. Birdsong. Was a light red with white points, noted as a superior fox dog and sire. One of the best dogs ever in my kennel.

MAUPIN'S MINNIE.—Small in size, white with black and tan spots, very compactly built, was noted for her great speed and endurance. Her grandsire and dam both by Colonel Maupin's celebrated dog Tennessee Lead.

THE KINSLOW BITCH was a full Birdsong and a fine fox dog.

TRIGG.—Black and tan, fine size, one of the best fox dogs of his day.

LEAD.—Black and tan, noted for his speed and endurance.

DALLAS.—White, black and tan spots. good dog.

JEPSON'S ANNIE.—Owned by Dr. J. J. Jepson, bred by George Haefer of Jefferson county, Kentucky. A dog of great speed and endurance, noted as being the dam of many fine fox dogs.

HAEFER'S BRENDA.—White, black and tan spots, purchased from Colonel Maupin and said to be one of the finest dogs of her day.

LITTLE ANNIE.—Bred in Georgia by Colonel Ward, whelped in my kennel in 1868. She was noted for her hunting qualities and was a fine fox hound. Her produce were all good dogs.

ROSE.— Bred and owned by Colonel Ward, sent me in whelp and returned. She was by the celebrated dog July and possessed many of his good qualities.

TENNESSEE CROWNER.—Was a very large black and tan dog brought from Tennessee by Sam Duncan, noted for his hunting and trailing qualities. This dog and Tennessee Lucian were very probably of the same parent stock as Mr. Maupin's famous Tennessee Lead.

KINSLOW'S IDA.—Black, medium size, one of the best foxhounds of her day, dam of many fine dogs.

FANNIE.—Red and tan, medium size and a good dog.

TRUMP.—Black and tan, white points, a fine hunter, very speedy and game.

ROCK.—Secured for a stud dog from Garrard county. Was white and black spotted, of good size. We lost him on the first hunt in a fox cave.

MERCY.—Was a full Maupin bitch, direct from Mr. Maupin's kennel.

HODO.—Was bred by Birdsong in 1853, black, white tips, 26 inches high.

There is an error in the chart of Dick's Dog; Jim Sibbins, was out of Fannie. Fannie was out of Della, by Trump, Trump was by Rock, out of Mercy. Rock and Mercy were full Maupin.

LOU.—Was full sister to Butler and came from Maryland. See description of Butler in chart of Longstreet.

BRUNETTE.—Was bred by Birdsong in 1856.

KIT.—Was a stray bitch, in Jones county.

HODO, JR.—Was bred by Ridgley and raised by Alexander.

NED.
Trooper—Mercy.

(From the Sportsman Review.)

THE FULL CRY PACK.

"Ancient history has been read,
And stories have been told
Of how Moss caught his mare,
It was in the days of old.
Oh, he was as cunning as a fox,
And as crafty as a hare,
And I'll tell you bye and bye
How Moss caught his mare."
—*From an Old Song.*

There is a demand just now for everything pertaining to field sports, and especially as regards the most exciting and healthful of them all—fox hunting.

The praises of favorite dogs have been sung until their names have become famous; but, while reading with interest and pleasure of the wonderful achievements of Hodo, July, Old Kate, and others, I have felt a desire to give to the lovers of sport something of the history of what I, at that time, considered the ideal hound—certainly one of the fastest and gamest of his kind. Recognizing my inability to do my favorite justice in print, I have taken every opportunity to recount the wonderful things Old Waxie accomplished to fellow sportsmen, around camp fires, or on any occasion where the subjects of the chase were being discussed. Having become thoroughly familiar with the history, if not worried with its repetition, my friends will no longer listen quietly to the telling of it, and will take themselves off the minute Old Waxie's name is mentioned. Having no one to tell it to now, I will endeavor to write an account of one of his many achievements for the benefit of those who never heard of or were so fortunate as to know this wonderful dog.

It was about the year '82. I had returned from college to spend the holidays and brought home with me a fellow student and chum. My friend had never been on a hunt; in fact, had been reared in a city, and his experience with horse and saddle was limited to a few rides around the suburbs of Memphis. He had read and heard of what great sport it was to ride to hounds, and a few days after our arrival, when I suggested we go for a day's hunt, he was delighted with the idea, and could scarcely eat or sleep in anticipation of the chase.

At that time I had no dogs myself, but had often gone with my uncles, H. C. and William F. Trigg, both of whom had famous packs of the Birdsong and Maupin strain of hounds, and I knew either would be glad to go or let me hunt their dogs. Uncle Will Trigg lived eight miles in the country, and when I spoke to Uncle Haiden about the proposed hunt, he suggested that I go that evening to his brother's and join himself and my friend the next morning about daybreak. The "Wade Cave" was to be the meeting place, a famous resort for the red fox, and at that time the home of an old red that had been in the habit of giving a pack of dogs about all they cared for before taking to earth. This cave was situated in deep woods, about midway between town and my uncle's place in the country. After arranging for Charlie Goodwin—my friend—to go to Uncle Haiden for the night, so as to be up for an early start, I mounted my horse about dark, and arrived at Uncle Will's for late supper. I told him the object of my visit, and he seemed delighted at the prospect of beating his brother's pack with "Trump" and "Polly," his two best dogs. There was between them the greatest rivalry as to the merits of their individual dogs, and though they had the same blood, and would combine their packs to defeat others, the question of which had the fastest dog was never satisfactorily settled. After seeing that his pack were securely shut up to prevent them from going out for a run on their own account that night, we turned in, but were up before any signs of daybreak. After a substantial breakfast of ham and eggs, corn cakes and a cup of strong coffee, we unkenneled and fed the dogs and started for the appointed meeting place. We had with us "Trump," a **magnificent speci-**

men of the Maupin strain, and his little mates, "Charlie," "Smoker" and "Jake." We also had two of Trump's get, out of a full Birdsong bitch, "Mel" and "Polly," about eighteen months old. "Trump" was at the head of the pack, but "Polly," though young, had shown unusual speed and gameness.

When within about a mile of the cave, and just as signs of day were appearing, "Trump," who had been leaping leisurely along in front of our horses, stopped short, and after listening for a second, went off down the road at full speed, followed by the rest of the dogs, but in silence. We reined up and could distinctly hear the pack of the other party in full cry about a mile and a half from us, and making for the cave a little to our left. We put spurs to our horses and ran for that point, but when half a mile from it we heard Trump and his mate "put in" ahead of the pursuing pack, and so close to the fox that he had evidently to take the cave or lose his life.

Both parties arrived there a few minutes later. Uncle Haiden was of the opinion that he had run upon a youngster on his return from a marauding expedition during the night, and that we would find the old runner in the big woods to the south of the cave, his favorite covert.

My friend Goodwin was in high glee, having enjoyed the short spin after the young fox immensely, and was anxious to jump one that would stand before the hounds longer.

Uncle Haiden had brought with him "Scott," "Trigg," "Waxie," "Wildgoose," "Rachel," "Bug," "Hornet," "One Eye," and "Wonder," all well trained and tried in many a hard race, where speed and gameness were tested to the utmost.

We lost little time, but started for the big woods, hoping to find the old fellow before the heavy frost of that night should be dried on leaves and grass by the morning sun. Between us and the big woods was a smaller clump of trees interspered with an undergrowth of briars and bushes. Before reaching these we heard the fierce challenge of "Trump," followed almost immediately by the cry of the entire pack, which went away so rapidly that we knew they were running, and close on the game. Feeling sure that they had unkenneled the old fox, we galloped rapidly to the top of the hill on the edge of the big woods in which direction the dogs had gone. They had already passed over the hill, and were a mile beyond, making for an old field of sage grass and briars, through which the fox always ran to the bluff of a creek beyond before returning.

Knowing where he would cross after his double on the bluff, we started to ride leisurely to the point. We had gone but a few hundred yards when we were surprised to hear the dogs returning over a route thick with bushes and fallen trees, and one the old red never took. They were dodging in among these rough places, but making such a cry as indicated they were close on their game, which was surely in distress and endeavoring to elude them by making short doubles. We were considerably mystified at such capers being cut by a fox that had more than once given us several hours of running in the open woods and fields before taking to earth.

We were not to remain in doubt long, however, for the dogs were now closer to us, and by the savage cry made we knew they were in sight of the fox, though sheltered from our view by the bushes. We watched with bated breath, expecting to see the fox break from the covert and make across the field to our right but instead we heard that peculiar cry made by the gray fox when caught. We knew then that we had been mistaken, and that we had caught some chance or stray gray fox that happened to be out of his accustomed haunts. This proved correct. Dismounting and making our way to the spot where they had stopped in the branches of a fallen tree, I found one of the largest gray dog foxes I ever saw. They had caught him in about twenty minutes run.

Though we had had two races, the sun was just showing, and we concluded to ride to the far edge of the woods where we knew we would find the trail of the old runner should he have been frightened from his covert by the cry of the pack after the gray. Sure enough, there we found where he had slipped out down a small branch lined with willows. The first challenge came from Scott this time, and was given in that clear, musical tone which, when repeated rapidly, as he gave it when on a warm trail, immediately brought every dog in his hearing to him and filled a sportsman's entire being with that indescribable feeling that always takes possession when he realizes the game in sight, the sport about to begin and certain to be good. The pack made for the bluff led by Scott, the others having all fallen in with the exception of Trump, who had made for the bluff at once, knowing that there he was sure to find the game. He did strike fully a hundred yards ahead, but his challenge, resembling the cry of a brant given rapidly, was known to the others and they immediately hearkened to him. The scent had freshened, and before they reached the top of a hill beyond the bluff where the fox had turned sharp to the left, they were well together and running on a hot trail. We rode to the upper end of the bluff and sighted the fox as he came down and crossed the creek and made up through the open woods. He did not seem particularly concerned regarding his future prospects in life. His gait was more of a leisurely gallop than a run. He carried his brush, which was well tipped with white, straight out behind, and being a very bright golden red, he presented a sight long to be remembered by those who saw him as he passed through the bright spots of forest made by the rays of the newly risen sun.

The dogs came about four hundred yards behind. Having their joints well limbered up in the two previous runs, they were setting a lively pace and one well calculated to soon remind Mr. Red that this was not his usual morning exercise. Trump was in the lead, which fact brought a cheering halloo to him from his master, but Scott, Trigg, Waxie, Wildgoose and Polly were well bunched close up, with the others yelping at their heels. The fox led through the woods and toward the Wade cave. We galloped behind to the road on the edge of the woods, and knowing that the old fellow was feeling too good to take to shelter so soon, the country intervening being very rough, we concluded to await the return. We heard the pack pass over the ridge and go into the deep hollow at the head of which was the cave.

They went out of our hearing and for a minute we feared he had gone in, but no. There's a cry; is it "Trump" or "Trigg?"—two men at least differ widely—followed by the full crying pack as they rise the hill beyond, and turn to the left circling for the return. They are two miles from us, but we can hear them distinctly. We know just where they will come into the field in front of us. They have gone six or seven miles and are warming to their work. They have certainly lessened the distance between them and the fox. Every nerve strung to the highest pitch, we sit in silence, our horses close together. Not a word is spoken, except when Uncle Will says something about "Watch for Trump to come over the fence first," which causes his brother to smile as if such a thing was impossible. The dogs are now in the woods where we unkenneled the gray, and the fox must soon show himself in the field. Yes, there he comes, on to the rail fence. He pauses just a second and glances back as if to satisfy himself he could make across the field without showing himself to his pursuers. He must have concluded there was little time to lose as he bounded off and with tremendous leaps made for the cover of the woods on the opposite side. We lose all interest in his foxship now, as we watch that panel of fence to see what dog comes over first. The woods ring with echoes, as the flying pack rush for the fence. They are there; "Scott" and "Trump" come over as if they were yoked together, so close that no advantage can be claimed for either by their respective owners; but "Trigg" and "Waxie." "Polly" and "Bug" are over and in the field almost as soon. The fox has left a blazing scent on the damp, dead grass of the pasture.

They run with heads up, giving tongue at every leap. They are all over the fence now and it is two hundred yards across the field. Here is a chance to test speed. We sit like statues and almost as quiet. "Trump" and "Scott" start across neck and neck. Neither can gain a hair's breadth on the other. I keep my eye on "Waxie;" I know this is the time for him. He has run long enough behind. Yes, he is gaining. He has passed "Trigg" and challenged the leaders. He has lapped them by half a length. "Waxie" is my favorite and I unconsciously urge my horse a step forward. His master is watching him, too, and reaches for his hat, which goes into the air with an ear-splitting yell which seems to lift the gallant fellow over the fence a full length in front of the leaders. We put spurs to the impatient horses who are as much enthused as their riders, and attempt to follow through the woods.

One might as well attempt to catch the shadow of a passing vulture; before we are to the branch they are on the bluff and the echoes which come back tell us with what confidence they are running. The fox doubles behind the top of the hill and turns our way. We look out for him, but he turns the crown of the hill once more, evidently afraid to trust himself to the open woods again. Old fellow, you have come to that bluff once too often and you begin to realize it when too late. You must do something. Here he comes down the bluff and across the creek, making a last desperate effort to reach the cave three miles away, where he has so often found shelter. Yes, there came Waxie—his peculiar "Ku-Ku" given with such fierce defiance to the flying pack twenty yards in his rear that I must rejoice with him. I let out a great "Halloo!" He looks up and catches sight of his game fifty years ahead. His mouth shuts like a jack-knife and we, sitting there on the bank of the stream, witness the greatest burst of speed ever seen. Before the fox is aware of his danger, the now silent Waxie is within ten steps of him. He hears his approaching feet, looks back and seems to abandon all hope of escape, for he suddenly turns and is caught between the glistening teeth of one of the fastest and gamest dogs that ever followed a horn.

GONE AWAY.

GLASGOW, KY., Feb. 22, 1895.

(From American Field.)

TWENTY-FOUR YEARS AGO.

BY FULL CRY.

Startled from a sound sleep by a loud knock at my chamber door, I heard a voice say:

"Hello, Marse Hade!"

"Who is that?"

"Me— Sam."

"What time is it, Sam?"

"Dunno, 'cept I knows it's 'bout time youse up. De mornin' stair's up, the chickens dun crow'd fur day, and ole Foris a-talkin' down ter de ken'l."

"Sam, what kind of a morning is it?"

"It's des de kine youse allers talkin' 'bout so much. De win's in de souf, an' de sky as cloudy. W'at you gwine ter ride, Marse Hade?"

"I guess I had better ride Black Fox, Sam."

"Dat 'pens on whar you gwine ter go."

"We will try the old fellow on the mountain this morning."

"Dem cliffs er monstrus high, en' de gullies er powerful deep. I spec' Wile Bill is de best hoss ter take dem leaps."

"All right, Sam, I will ride Wild Bill, and you can ride Black Fox."

"No sar, wid yo' purmission I'm gwine ter ride ole Gab-

FULL CRY HOUNDS.

'rell"—a mule—"heze sho-footed en can go inter de deepes' gullies, and clime de steepes' mountins, en neber fall wid dis nigger."

"All right, you can ride Gabe. Wake Eliza and tell her to get us a cup of coffee."

"Lor', Marse Hade, Lize bin up fo' de mornin' stair en dun got eve'ything reddy. She dun cooked de pa'tridges and got de coffee bilin'."

"All right, I will be down in a few minutes."

While at the breakfast table, enjoying quail on toast, soft boiled eggs and a cup of coffee, Sam entered.

"Marse Hade, Ize dun fed de hosses and give de dorgs sump'n fer to stay der stummucks, coz dey go'nter have de wurk cut out fer dem terday. Yo' 'aint got nun dat old corn juice, have you, Marse Hade? It wud help dis nigger pow'fully."

"There is the bottle, Sam, help yourself; here is some sugar."

"Great Jehoserfac, Marse Hade, Sam ain't gwine ter never spile medicine like dis wid nuffin."

"All right, Sam; eat your breakfast quick, then get the horses and let us be off."

"Yes, sah."

While enjoying a Partaga I inquired of Sam what hounds we should take.

"Well, sah, fus en formus we must take de ole Gen'ril"—meaning Forest—"den Whitefoot, Cricket, Chase, Bee, Money, Baby, Rip, Minnie en Matt."

"What about Fannie, Sam?"

"She wus lame, an' de pups can't keep in her'n dis'unce after dat ole trav'ler."

"All right. Let the others out."

And out they came, ten as game and fleet fox-hounds as ever followed me to the field, trained and drilled like a company of soldiers. After expressing their delight by a few yelps, as if to say "good morning," we were off to the grounds, eight miles distant. I looked at my watch; it was 4:10 a. m.

Wild Bill and Gabe were enthused as much as riders and hounds. We went at a slow gallop, and the hounds knew full well where they were going. They kept close up, going neither to right nor left, and not a sound from one of them.

"Ride up, Sam. Sam, I intend to beat the General this morning."

"No, sah. Dat dorg nev'r did live what cud shake his tail in ole Foris' face."

"Yes, I think Baby and Chase can do it to-day."

"No, sah, dey nev'r will git ole 'nuf fer dat."

I struck a match and looked at my watch. It was just 5:20 and growing brighter in the east. We had reached the grounds, and not a hound had left the road.

"Now, Sam, go down to the cave"—distant half a mile—"and remain there until you hear the horn. Don't let him in."

It was the custom of this fox after standing up from one to three hours to take to this, and only this, cave. I was determined that morning to kill him or make him find another burrow.

After Sam had had time to get to the cave I gave the word and the pack was off. I rode up on the knob (though called a mountain), and when I reached the top not a hound was in sight or to be heard. It was indeed a typical morning for the sport; a gentle breeze from the south, the ground damp from recent rains, the last of November, and all things favorable. I struck a match to light a cigar, and looked at my watch; it was 5:40, when hark! the first challenge comes from Chase (the son of old Longstreet). It was daylight by now, and Baby answered two hundred yards to the left. Every hound knew when Baby spoke it was time to be getting there, for the game was not far off. Forest now challenged, still to the left and repeated rapidly, as much as to say, "We are off, fall into line and follow." Chase was already with him. Baby moved up, followed by the gallant little Minnie with her clear tenor notes that seemed to lend wings to Whitefoot and

Cricket as they passed me at breakneck speed and soon spoke out. Money also joined them. Bee was there, and Mattie. Yes, and then Rip, with his deep bass accompaniment. I dismounted, girthed my saddle tighter, and examined stirrups and bridle, for I knew the ride was to be hard and the route rough. I had followed the same fox a dozen times before.

The scent was growing warmer every minute, and each hound was now playing well its part. I knew each and every mouth as well as Theodore Thomas knew the instruments in his orchestra. The pack emerged from the woods and entered a large field, in the center of which were twenty or thirty acres of briars and bushes, and I rode rapidly to the far side in time to see the fox slip out. The hounds were now in the bushes; now they reached the spot, here they come, with heads up and sterns down, running as if they were in sight instead of being four or five hundred yards from their game, and away they go into another body of woods. Knowing where the fox would double and cross back I rode to the point and listened. Yes, they are coming. After a few minutes he comes in sight, his brush extended and looking like a staff of gold tipped with ivory; and here comes the gallant pack, all up, each and every hound doing his best for the trail (I was glad Sam was not there, for Forest was slightly in the lead). They had gained very little, if any, on the fox, and off to the right of the knob they went. I rode rapidly to the left and near the cave. Then I heard them swing around toward me. The fox saw me, however, and swung to my left, and I failed to see either fox or pack, but they went near enough to Sam for him to see the hounds.

I put spurs to my horse and was going to where the fox unkenneled, when I heard: "Oh! hole on dar, Marse Hade!" I looked back and saw Sam on Gabriel coming at breakneck speed, and I called out:

"Stop, Sam. Where are you going?"

"No whar, sah. I jess want'r tell de God's trufe."

"Well, what do you want to tell?"

"Well, sah, 'fo' God it's de trufe."

"What is it? Tell me and go back to the cave."

"Well, Marse Hade, I'm de li'ness nigger ever wuz ef Foris wuz'nt fli'n'."

"Well, weren't the other hounds flying too?"

"Yes, dey wuz, but Foris wuz fli'n' de hi'es'. Den Baby en Whitefoot en al'em; but dey never will shake der tails in Foris' face."

I lost five minutes with Sam, and failing to see them through the field I made for the point where I saw him on his return. I could hear them coming. There he goes, over the same line! And here comes the pack. They had gained considerably, and the fox was not three hundred yards to the good. (Glad again that Sam was not present.) The hounds were all well bunched and were running to kill. Away I went with them, though not saying a word (silence is the first qualification of a true sportsman), and for two miles I rode behind them. Forest was still leading, with Whitefoot second, Money, Chase Minnie and Baby bunched; and Rip, Cricket and Mattie from fifty to one hundred yards to the rear.

I swung round the knob and turned the fox from the cave. Sam failed to see fox or hounds but called out as I passed him:

"How is dey makin' hit?"

"I will beat Forest yet. Stay at the cave."

"Dey'll never shake der tails in dat ole dorg's face."

Over the fence into the field came the hounds, and in about the same positions, except that Baby had moved up to second place and was close to Forest. I now went to the opposite side of the field, and along he came, his brush no longer carried defiantly in the air; he carried it low down now, as he went into the woods, the pack evidently gaining. The hounds followed into the woods, and the fox doubled and re-entered the twenty acres of briars and bushes. There the pack was within one hundred yards of him. I galloped to the opposite side, expecting him to make for the cave; though he doubled among the briars, a sure sign he was in trouble. Out he came and only half a mile to the cave. He entered the woods, and then commenced the race for life.

As the pack passed me I gave the first halloo. Then I charged the fence and got over all right. I could see, though, the pack had not yet caught sight of the fox. To the cave he went, and I wished he could get in this time; but Sam kept him out, and he made for the top of the knob. The pack was now in sight and must soon kill. They passed over the top of the knob and stopped. Riding to the spot, instead of a dead fox I found he had taken refuge in the root of an immense poplar tree.

Up came Sam on Gabe, screaming like a madman, and falling from his mule he seized Forest in his arms.

"I tole you so. Yes, sah, I did. I'se seed hit befo'en I no'd I'd see hit ergin terday!"

"What did you tell me, Sam?"

"Dat dar wuz no livin' dorg what cud shake his tail in ole Foris' face."

"Sam, what shall we do?"

"Marse Hade, old Foris dun beat dis fox on de squar' en he mus' tase his blood."

Unlike the English sportsman, I could not resist the temptation to bolt this fox. He had been fairly beaten and I agreed with Sam that the gallant pack should enjoy their hard-earned victory. I suggested that we let Minnie (she being small enough to enter the hole) go in and drive him out.

But instead, the fox drove her out with a badly lacerated and bloody face.

"What shall we do now, Sam?"

"Let's put Min and Bee bofe in, en dey'll fetch' im."

"All right, Sam; let them go."

In Minnie went with Bee and the fight was renewed, lasting ten or fifteen minutes, when the brave little bitches came out, dragging with them the dead fox. Upon examination I found the toenails of this fox had been worn off by the frequent long runs I had given him.

GLASGOW, KY.

www.ingramcontent.com/pod-product-compliance
Lightning Source LLC
Chambersburg PA
CBHW031121160426
43192CB00008B/1064